MODERN TIMES

Franco and the Spanish Civil War

Titles in this series

MODERN TIMES

Franco and the Spanish Civil War

L. E. Snellgrove
HEAD OF HISTORY DEPARTMENT, DE STAFFORD SCHOOL, CATERHAM

LONGMAN

LONGMAN GROUP LIMITED
London
Associated companies, branches and representatives throughout the world
© L.E. Snellgrove 1965

First published 1965
Seventh impression 1980
ISBN 0 582 20422 4

Printed in Hong Kong by
Sheck Wah Tong Printing Press Ltd

Acknowledgements

We are grateful to Messrs. Martin Secker & Warburg Ltd and Harcourt, Brace &
World, Inc. for permission to include an extract from *Homage to Catalonia* by George
Orwell.

For permission to reproduce photographs we are grateful to the following: Associated Press—pages 28, 53, 57, 64, 77 top, and 86; Barnaby's Picture Library—page 127;
Camera Press—page 119; Fox Photos—page 71; Gernsheim Collection—page 23;
Keystone Press—pages 39, 60, 79 and 103; Museo del Prado—page 10; Paul Popper
—pages 30, 35, 37, 45, 62, 67 and 78; Pictorial Press—pages 69 and 121; Radio Times
Hulton Picture Library—pages 19, 24, 26 and 27; Robert Capa—Magnum Photos—
pages 59, 77 bottom, 84, 90, 105, 110, 113 and 117; Servicio Informativo Español
—page 99; United Press International (UK) Limited—page 94; Visnews Limited—
page 46. The painting photographed on page 97 is on extended loan to The Museum
of Modern Art, New York, from the artist, P. Picasso.

The maps, with the exception of those on pages 3 and 11, are based on some in *The
Spanish Civil War* by Hugh Thomas, by permission of Eyre and Spottiswoode (Publishers) Limited, and Harper and Row, Publishers Incorporated.

Preface

A civil war is a national disaster. It divides countries, states and towns, splits even villages and causes brother to fight brother, father to kill son. Men wage it with extra bitterness because it is a family quarrel. Few wars of modern times have seen such ferocious brutality as the Spanish Civil War. To this day the wounds are not healed and only a new generation, born since it ended, is likely to forget what their fathers did.

As a war it was a strange mixture of old and new, poised like a bridge between the trench fighting of the First World War and the mechanized 'total' war of the Second. Often in its battles men advanced to the sound of bugles or took part in cavalry charges. In the mountains the Carlist bands crawled forward over rough ground clutching their rifles as their ancestors had done a hundred years before. Yet its losses were enormous, dwarfed only by the gigantic deathroll of two world wars. Its tanks and bombers, its systematic executions, its refugees and its propaganda were part of the paraphernalia of a modern war.

More modern still were the political beliefs of those involved. Although it began as a Spanish quarrel the rival powers of Europe magnified and distorted its real aims, injecting their own hatreds into the situation. Hitherto Communists and Fascists had fought in the streets of cities with sticks and stones; in Spain, organized as large armies, they were able to close in a death grip. At Guadalajara the arrogant and successful Fascists suffered their first defeat. In Barcelona and other cities the Communists exercised a ruthless control to be repeated in many countries after 1945. Spain became a mirror in which thoughtful Europeans could see their terrible future.

No civil war has created so much outside interest. All over the world men took sides; only the Bomb has created so much argument and concern in more recent times. To some Franco was a hero, saving Spain from Communism. To some he was a Fascist dictator enslaving his own people. To a few, including Britons, the argument could not be solved by words alone. They went to Spain and fought for their beliefs.

If this book helps you to understand why they did this it will have achieved its purpose.

L. E. Snellgrove

Contents

1 Prologue

The flight to Tetuan[1]

On a sunny day in July 1936 three men, two Spaniards and an Englishman, sat down to lunch in a restaurant in the Strand, London. They wanted privacy and asked the waiter for a table where they could not be overheard. During their meal one of the Spaniards explained why he had invited the Englishman out to lunch. His reason was a surprising one.

'I want a man and three platinum blondes to fly to Africa tomorrow,' he announced.

For a time the Englishman was too surprised to speak. 'Must there really be three?' he asked eventually in mystified tones.

The Spaniard thought about this.

'Well, perhaps two would be enough,' he admitted.

The · Englishman, a publisher named Douglas Jerrold, wanted to help his friend. That same day he remembered a man who might be able to arrange such a flight. An old friend, Major Hugh Pollard, was an adventurer who as a journalist had reported wars and revolutions in various parts of the world. Sure enough, Pollard's only reaction when asked over the telephone whether he would fly to Africa was, 'Depends on the girls!'

'You can choose,' explained Jerrold, and added: 'The aeroplane may be stolen when you get there. In that case you come back by boat.'

This strange remark made Pollard more interested than ever. He invited the Spaniards and Jerrold to his home in Sussex. Here, in the peaceful summer countryside, they planned a flight which would take them to a very different part of the world, to the sands and heat of the Canary Islands. The usual travel problems, how to get passports, money, and so forth were arranged quickly. Blondes were a more difficult matter! Where could they find two girls prepared to act as if

[1] Based on Douglas Jerrold, *Georgia Adventure*, Collins, 1937.

they were tourists, girls who might be stranded in a hostile country? Pollard asked his daughter Diana to come and she agreed. But what of the other girl? Diana remembered a friend, Dorothy Watson, who might be interested. The men jumped in a car and sped to Dorothy's home, only to find that she was out delivering chickens! After touring the dusty lanes for a while, she was found and persuaded to take part in the adventure. Last, but far from least, Pollard was sure he knew a pilot who would fly them, Captain Bebb of Olley Airways Ltd. Within hours the plot had been hatched. Dressed and equipped as holiday-makers the travellers were to go to the Canary Islands where their plane would be stolen by someone who needed to get to Morocco quickly. Dorothy and Diana had read of such exciting situations. They had never expected to take part in one.

On 11 July 1936 Captain Bebb took off from Croydon Airport with his passengers in a fast Dragon Rapide aircraft bound for Las Palmas. The solitary plane, rising swiftly above the houses of suburban Surrey that summer afternoon, probably caused no one a second thought. Possibly the excited 'tourists' themselves could scarcely have realized the significance of what they were doing. At Las Palmas they were regarded as typically crazy English people who had arrived without official permission. One local man was annoyed. 'It's just like the English to land here without papers,' he grumbled, 'they think they own the earth; I shall remove the propeller after dark.'

He did not carry out his threat and the plane was still in one piece at dawn on 18 July when a small man, carrying a brown paper parcel, came on board with his wife, daughter and two friends. After a very few words of greeting, he seated himself with the parcel on his knee. Captain Bebb clambered into the cockpit and took off, leaving Pollard and the two girls to pretend they had been stranded. The plane headed for Tetuan in North Africa where it arrived twenty-four hours later after two stops. As it circled over the town at seven o'clock in the morning its chief passenger opened his parcel which contained the uniform of a Spanish general. When the Rapide taxied to a halt he was no longer dressed as a civilian. Army officers rushed forward to greet him as their leader. He gave them a

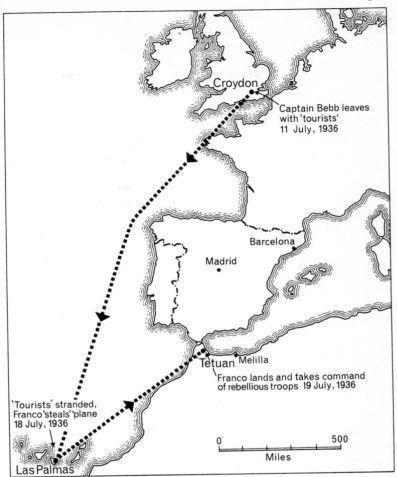

The flight to North Africa.

slogan, 'Blind faith in victory'. Then they hurried off leaving Captain Bebb to wonder what exactly it was all about.

Perhaps the tremendous news from the outside world had already filtered through to him. Perhaps he knew that the man with the brown paper parcel had rebelled against his Government, and that fighting had begun in Spain. Perhaps he knew that his name was General Francisco Franco. What he could not have known was that a three-year war had just

3

started which would cost the lives of 600,000 people. Or that his passenger, after winning that war, would be the dictator of Spain. Rarely can one aeroplane flight and a whispered conversation over lunch have played such an important part in a nation's history.

Before he boarded the plane that morning Franco had broadcast a long manifesto to the Spanish people, 'Spaniards!' he announced. 'To whomever feels a holy love to Spain, to those who in the ranks of the army and navy have made professions of faith in the service of the country, to those who have sworn to defend her from her enemies, the Nation calls you to her defence. . . .'[1] Later his words made it clear that he regarded the nation's 'enemies' as the Spanish Government. Thousands of workers in Madrid, Barcelona and other cities disagreed with the general, and regarded him as the enemy who had come to destroy their liberty. The result was a terrible war which ruined Spain, and which has caused argument ever since. 'Who was wrong?' people have asked. The Nationalists led by Franco and the other generals? Or the Republican Government led by men like Azaña, Caballero and Negrin?

There is no easy answer to this question because civil wars are never easy to explain. Countries usually go to war with each other for simple reasons, for trade, for conquest, for increased power. Many quarrels are needed to divide a nation, to make one province or political party fight another, to split families so that father fights son and brother turns upon brother. Such a tragedy must have a long history of jealousy, unfairness and hatred behind it. It is rare that one side is right and the other wrong, although we may feel that one fought for better reasons than the other.

Of all civil wars few have had so many causes as the Spanish catastrophe and none has roused quite so much interest in the outside world. England's Civil War was hardly noticed by other European countries because they were fighting their own Thirty Years War. No foreign power joined in the American Civil War. The Spanish conflict, however, occurred when

[1] Translated by S. F. A. Coles in *Franco of Spain*, Spearman, 1954.

Europe was in uproar with some countries preparing openly for war. Political beliefs were everywhere causing trouble. Fascists and Nazis hated Communists; the western democracies, France, Britain and the U.S.A., disliked both. Consequently when Spain was torn by civil war outsiders judged it by their own quarrels. Communist Russia helped the Republicans and so they were called Communists. Nazi Germany and Fascist Italy helped Franco and so he was called a Fascist. In fact, Franco and the other rebellious generals fought for varied reasons. Caballero and Negrin were not Communists and their followers were so disunited that they frequently fought each other. Unfortunately it was easier to say that it was a war between Fascists and Communists than to try to unravel the real reasons for the struggle.

These went back a long way and involved conflicting beliefs and difficult problems. The flight to Tetuan helped to start a war. It also brought to the boil hatreds resulting from nearly one hundred and fifty years of trouble in Spain.

2 Spanish Problems

Early history

Spain is inhabited by varied and defiant people. Foreigners think of them as Spaniards but they call themselves Castilians, Aragónese, Andalusians, Catalans or Basques, just as the British refer to English, Welsh or Scots. Like these British races, each feels different from the other. Some speak their own language; all have distinct customs. Unlike the Welsh or Scots, however, these Spanish people want to rule themselves, to be separate from each other, in a way which is almost unknown in Britain. Their attitude towards kings and princes who wanted a united Spain has always been rebellious. When the people of Aragón promised loyalty they did so with these words:

'We who are as good as you swear to you who are not better than we, to accept you as our king and sovereign lord provided you accept all our liberties and laws; but if not, not.'

Such an independent attitude can be seen in their traditional dress. The Basque with his red sash, the Andalusian in his short velvet jacket, or the Aragónese with his light blue stockings are all visible signs of this longing to be different. Even two matadors, when they enter the bullring, make sure they are out of step!

Such separatism, as it is called, is due partly to history, partly to geography. A glance at a map of Spain will show large mountain ranges cutting slantwise across the land, dividing it into smaller areas. The Basques in their narrow mountain valleys, the Catalans basking in the Mediterranean sun, the Galicians on their windswept Atlantic coast, are different because they live in different surroundings. A map of Europe will reveal more. This rugged peninsula is a bridge between Europe and Africa, the northern frontier formed by the Pyrenees mountains, the southern by the Straits of Gibraltar. Such an exposed position has caused it to be invaded from opposite directions and by various races. From the north have come the Romans and Visigoths; from the south Carthaginians and Moors. In Christian times the Moors drove deep into Spain, establishing a 'wonderful Arab civilization with its centre at Cordoba. This division between two peoples and two faiths lasted from 711 until 1492. The Basques, the Franks of Catalonia and the kingdoms of Galicia, Asturias and Castile managed to stay unconquered. Along the frontier Christian kings built castles; the name Castile means 'land of castles'. When the Christians felt strong enough to invade Moorish territory, this *Reconquista*, or reconquest, divided Spain still further because the princes who led the Crusaders carved out more kingdoms for themselves. Navarre, Castile and Barcelona became independent. Portugal, protected by mountains and able to get English assistance from the sea, began her own history.

These events had other results. In the south, Spanish music, Spanish architecture, Spanish ways of life were influenced by the Arabs long after the last Moorish army had been driven into the sea. In northern and central Spain the knights who had fought this 'holy war' became intolerant of non-Christians. Persecution of them grew into a cruel habit, and Christian Spain celebrated her new freedom in 1492 by expelling the Jews. In a way faith became a symbol of unity, a badge to show you were in the right army. Not to be a Christian was to be a traitor. This idea has been common in Spain ever since.

It was encouraged by rulers who realized that religion was something all parts of Spain shared. Isabella of Castile and Ferdinand of Navarre, the first monarchs of a united Spain, deliberately used religion to bind their subjects together. They treated it with devotion and respect, so much so that Isabella was nicknamed 'the Catholic'. Their successors in the sixteenth century did the same. Inquisition courts in most Catholic states were set up to try people who offended against the laws of the Church. They punished witchcraft and heresy. In Spain, however, they did far more. The Inquisition, consisting of ten regional courts and helped by 20,000 'familiars' or spies who reported offenders, was practically a department of government. In Aragón, for instance, it was the only court which represented the King. With its help the Spanish

7

monarchs created a national Church which often ignored the Pope, and dominated the people.

At first this proudly independent organization, so typical of the Spanish character, flourished and produced fine thinkers and teachers. By the eighteenth century it had become isolated from progress. In 1773, for example, Salamanca university taught nothing about the theories of Isaac Newton who had lived nearly a hundred years before. Instead its students continued the medieval habit of arguing about what language the angels spoke and whether the sky was made of metal! Furthermore, a Church so closely linked with the government tended to be hated if the government itself was unpopular. Later we shall see the terrible results of this.

Spain and the Counter-Reformation

As the Catholic rulers struggled with their defiant subjects, the discoveries of Columbus and others gave Spain an empire larger than that of Rome. At its greatest extent, and during the short time the Spanish kings ruled Portugal, it comprised south Italy, Holland, Belgium, Portugal and part of France, Tunis, part of Morocco, all south and central America and parts of North America, the Philippines, Madeira, the Azores, Cape Verde, Guinea, the Congo, Angola, Mozambique, Ceylon, Borneo, Sumatra and the Moluccas. Only the British Empire has ever equalled it in size. At the same time France, Spain's chief enemy in Europe, was defeated on the battlefields of Italy.

Such vast possessions gave a misleading impression of power. Spain was mighty at that time, but not strong enough to cope successfully with the enormous problems of her empire when she was scarcely a united nation herself. Too much Spanish wealth was in expendable things like gold and silver, too little in thriving trade and growing industries. The turning point came in the sixteenth century. Protestant revolts against the Pope were everywhere leading to wars. Spain's Catholic kings, Charles V and later Philip II, felt it their duty to fight for the Pope. They put Spain at the head of what was called the Counter-Reformation. Year after year Spanish armies and fleets tried to defeat the Protestant powers, England, Holland and the north German states. The task was too great and they failed. Every British boy and girl knows how the Spanish Armada sailed to defeat in 1588. Few know that there were other armadas which suffered similar disasters. Meanwhile the huge empire was being attacked and its treasure stolen by Englishmen like Sir Francis Drake and Dutchmen like Piet Heyn.

By 1700 Spain was a weak country, worn out defending the Catholic faith. No more were her soldiers the terror of Europe; her proud fleets no longer sailed the seas in safety. When her King died leaving no child other European monarchs quarrelled amongst themselves over who should succeed him and sent troops to fight on the soil of Spain itself. A long war, famous for the victories of the Duke of Marlborough, settled the matter in favour of a Frenchman of the Bourbon family, Philip V. Because of this, Spain found herself fighting with France against Britain on many occasions in the eighteenth century. The Spanish empire was assaulted by British ships. Defeat followed defeat until in 1805 the last really powerful Spanish fleet was destroyed at Trafalgar, fighting bravely against Nelson. Wounded British sailors from this battle were amazed to find that Spaniards in Cadiz treated them as friends and the French as enemies. This was because French control was bitterly resented by such a proud people.

The final insult came when Napoleon's troops marched into Spain to attack Portugal. They had been invited by the Spanish King, Charles IV, but he was forced to abdicate. On 2 May 1808 the people of Madrid, led by three young officers, rose in revolt. What followed is shown in the grim paintings of Goya, the Spanish artist. Hundreds of patriots were shot by French firing squads or cut down by French cavalry. In revenge the furious Spaniards declared war, led by their priests and soldiers. At Baylen they inflicted the very first defeat upon Napoleon's troops. Then the British were asked to help and after six years of hard campaigning, Wellington, aided by Spanish and Portuguese, drove the French back across the Pyrenees.

The price paid for such a victory was heavy. 'The Spanish people', says one historian, 'shed its blood in torrents . . . commerce, industry and agriculture were ruined.' And although the French armies retreated they left behind the ideas

2

'Hundreds of patriots were shot by French firing squads.' A scene from Goya's painting 'The Horrors of War'.

of greater freedom and more equality, Liberal ideas as they are called, which the French revolutionaries had preached. These ideas led most of the Spanish colonists to revolt against Spanish rule and to break with the mother country. By 1830 much of the once proud empire had been lost. Worst still, these ideas had helped to divide the Spanish people.

A backward country drifts apart

The Spanish Church had become backward and old-fashioned in her ideas. Amidst the ruin of war, the Spanish people now discovered that a similar lack of progress in trade and industry had caused other countries to leave them behind. This was because agriculture was no longer the main source of a nation's wealth. A development of machinery on a large scale, an industrial revolution as it is called, was changing people's way of life all over Europe. No doubt you know something of Britain's industrial changes. Made rich by trade and assisted by inventions like the steam engine, she began to make goods of all kinds and sell them. Craftsmen's shops, which produce a few handmade articles, became less important. They were replaced by large factories, producing thousands of identical objects. This change from man to engine production led eventually to the high standard of comfort which some countries enjoy today.

By contrast Spain has remained an agricultural country, with only a limited industrial revolution. Two regions only, the iron and steel foundries of Bilbao province in the Basque country and the textile mills around Barcelona, were developed in a modern way. Unfortunately, Spanish governments, mainly composed of landowners, did not encourage even these areas to sell abroad whilst at home people were too poor to buy much of what was produced. For example, Bilbao in the nineteenth century made seven times as much iron as Spain could use, and Catalonia could supply all her textile needs with four months' work. Consequently the Spanish peasant remained as poor as his ancestor in the Middle Ages. The Spanish worker although slightly better off received far less than his European brothers.

Such backwardness affected men's minds as well as their

bodies. Spanish Liberals, talking and writing about more liberty, more fairness, better education for all and so on, received little encouragement from a starving people, who were more interested in a good meal than whether they voted or not. In other countries, wealth was gradually being divided more evenly, with millions of middle-class people who were neither very rich nor very poor. This class was able to fight the rich and improve conditions for the poor. In Spain, on the other hand, the workers and peasants ignored the few middle-class Liberals who wished to help them. They remained apart, dreaming of separatism for their region, or merely feeding their hatred of all government. Spain became a deeply divided nation. Rich and poor glared at each other across a deep rift in which the few Liberals were stranded helplessly. This fact is the key to the Spanish tragedy and helps to explain much later bloodshed.

Church versus Liberals

Whilst still at war against Napoleon the Spanish Liberals met at Cadiz and devised a Constitution, or form of government, separating Church from State, establishing free elections and giving the vote to most men. The King who returned two years later, Ferdinand VII, detested these suggestions. Instead he ruled like a dictator. Liberal politicians, unable to get much support from the people for the reasons already mentioned, turned for help to the army, many of whose officers came from Liberal families. Plotting against the King became widespread, made easier because many of the conspirators were freemasons. The society called Freemasonry seems first to have been organized in Spain by an English lord in 1728. Its secret ceremonies were especially hated by the Church for they seemed to imitate religious services. Because of this, men who resented the Church's power often became freemasons. Unfortunately, such a small, secret organization could never include the people. This is another reason why middle-class Liberals in Spain failed to get mass support.

With the soldiers against him Ferdinand's position grew unsafe. The army was at the height of its glory. It had fought bravely for six years; its leaders were experienced warriors. When it did act, at dawn on 1 January 1820, there was little chance of failure. Ferdinand was so unpopular that hardly anybody was prepared to fight for him. Rafael del Riego, the army leader, was able to win with a force which at the end consisted of forty-five men! This was the first time the army interfered in politics. It was not the last. Ever since, sometimes on the side of Liberals, sometimes on the side of those who wanted no changes, its officers have rebelled and altered the government by force.

Ferdinand was restored to the throne by the French. When he died in 1833 he left a will stating that his wife Cristina and daughter Isabella were to rule after him. Immediately a bitter struggle broke out which has influenced Spanish politics to this day. The Salic Law, observed in many countries at that time, prevented women from reigning alone. Consequently some Spaniards wanted Ferdinand's brother, Don Carlos, as King. The Carlists, as they were called, revolted against Cristina, supported by Aragón, Catalonia and the Basques. After five years' cruel warfare they were defeated and Carlos fled abroad. But Carlism has lived on because it believes in far more than a particular prince, or branch of the royal family. Don Carlos was devoted to the Church and he hated the Liberals. The motto of his followers was 'The King, Christ, and the Holy Virgin'. Their army was a crusading one, fighting the Church's battles against her enemies.

The clash between those who loved the Church as she was and those who wanted her reformed had begun twenty years before. In 1814 the Church had seemed as powerful as ever. Her doctrines went unchallenged, her massive cathedrals occupied dominant positions in every Spanish city, her parish churches were the centre of village life. She owned nearly twice as much land as the King whilst her priests were to be found in greater numbers than in any other Catholic country. There was, however, another side to the picture. The priests who fought in the Peninsular War did so for the old kings and the old ways. To men dreaming of more liberty, republican government and education free of the Church, they offered no encouragement at all. Indeed, when the war ended many Liberals were horrified to discover that some important churchmen wanted more power, not less. One bishop, for instance, made himself head of a provincial government.

The revolutionary Liberals of 1812 and 1820, although they described Roman Catholicism as 'the sole religion' of Spain, set about reducing the Church's power. Primarily this meant seizing its property, disentailing as it is called. Church land was put up for sale, all monasteries were closed and the pay of clergymen reduced. Some monastery buildings were turned into museums. At Málaga one was converted into a bullring. These drastic changes, which reduced some priests to the level of beggars, had three disastrous effects. First, Liberals had hoped that the large monastic estates would be bought by many small farmers. Unfortunately the opposite happened. Rich landowners purchased most of them and so made their large plantations larger. Second, the Church could only hope to have her power and property restored by the rich men who hated the Liberals. She decided to befriend the rich and to become interested in matters which have nothing to do with religion. Her leaders were often plotters, seeking violent political changes. They supported Don Carlos, encouraging priests to fight with their bands and nuns to make cartridges for their weapons. Later, her representatives became businessmen. They bought shares in industrial firms on such a scale that in the twentieth century the Spanish Church was described as 'the richest shareholder in the country'. As a result millions of Spaniards gradually rejected Church control and gave up being Christians. The first murder of a priest took place in 1834, probably as a reaction against Carlism. Since then priest killing and church burning have become peculiar Spanish customs.

This very first killing, which took place in a town, indicated another side to Carlism. Townsfolk were generally against the Church but a certain proportion of countryfolk were not. Carlism was in many ways a country movement, drawing its support from the hilly regions of northern Spain. In those parts the peasants disliked the progress and bustle of city life. Often they looked back with admiration to what they regarded as the ideal life of the Middle Ages. The Carlist wars, according to one historian, were 'a rebellion of pious countryfolk against corrupt and immoral city life'. In this battle between those who loved the old and the new, no large town ever went Carlist and none was ever captured by their armies. In the second war Carlist bands destroyed trains and railway stations just because they were new.

The dislike of Liberals for Churchmen and townsmen for country people was just as strong in 1936, when the Civil War started, as it had been a hundred years before when Zumala-carregui, the Carlist leader, was killed besieging Bilbao and priests were murdered in the streets of Madrid.

Army rule

For thirty years following the Carlist defeat in 1839 Spain was ruled by Queens Cristina and Isabella. The real rulers, how-ever, were the army and its generals. Some of these, like Espartero, were Liberals. Others, like Narváez, did not believe in greater freedom. They restored the Church's power by signing a Concordat, or agreement, with the Pope, reopened the monasteries and ruled as dictators. The army itself had far more officers than is usual, partly because all Carlist officers were allowed to join it if they wished. It was, in a sense, a political party with weapons.

Encouraged by their military leaders, Spanish Governments began to send the army off on foreign campaigns. Neither at home nor abroad was this scheme successful. In 1859 General O'Donnell invaded Morocco and after battles costing seven thousand lives seemed to have conquered this troublesome land. Unhappily he had really roused a hornet's nest. The Moors continued to ambush, torture and kill even when tem-porarily defeated in battle. Spain was forced to spend money on African expeditions until 1927. O'Donnell's second military adventure in Santo Domingo failed more quickly. After a speedy occupation which seemed to settle the matter, the South Americans revolted and drove the Spaniards out.

These defeats were not caused by cowardice. Spanish troops fought bravely but their equipment was out of date, their supplies poor. Dishonest generals, dishonest politicians and their friends made fortunes out of army contracts. Junior officers copied their superiors and sold rifles to the Moors. Consequently, Spain's nineteenth-century army of 90,000 men cost as much as the 500,000 strong armies of France and Italy! The peasants and workers knew of this and could see little point in heavy taxes for expensive armies and wasteful wars.

There was another even more important reason why the army was hated by ordinary men. At home it was used to hold down the starving peasantry. If trouble threatened a province would be put under military control. The local Captain-General, often a ruthless man, would execute or imprison all who demanded better conditions. In this unpopular work, another armed force, the Civil Guard, helped. Originally formed by Narváez in 1844, these guards were supposed to suppress bandits. Actually they were the open enemy of the people, forbidden to associate with the local inhabitants and forced to go around in twos for greater safety. Even their homes were small fortified posts in the countryside. The sight of their green uniforms, old-fashioned three-cornered hats and rifles became a common one in Spain. The peasants eyed them with silent hate and called them 'The Pair'.

The army and Civil Guard were grim watchdogs, ever ready to pull a trigger. They were the price Spain had to pay for an unfair land system.

The disease of the latifundia

Spain is chiefly an agricultural country. For centuries her farmers specialized in keeping sheep. The high plateaus of Castile, called the Meseta from the Spanish word for table, were dotted with wandering flocks which trampled upon the peasant's fields and crops. Each autumn it was a common sight to see huge dust clouds hanging in the air as the sheep were driven down to Estremadura. By the mid-eighteenth century good corn land was overgrown with palmetto and because few men are needed to look after sheep it was possible to ride for days without seeing a house. In the nineteenth century came a change. Revolutions tended to be won by landowners, who were more interested in growing crops than keeping sheep. So flocks were discouraged by constant ploughing, communally owned land was sold by government order, and two products, wheat and olives, were given an importance they have kept to this day.

If such farms had been owned by a fair proportion of the people all would have been well. Unfortunately this was not the case. In certain areas, such as Old and New Castile, Estremadura, Andalusia and La Mancha, trouble arose because of what are termed *latifundia*, that is, farms which were much too large. Enormous estates developed, owned by rich families who hired labourers or left large areas uncultivated. In Seville in the nineteenth century, for example, 5 per cent of the people owned 72 per cent of the province's farming land; in Cadiz 3 per cent owned 67 per cent. Deprived of the meadows upon which they might have reared a pig or some poultry, unable to afford to own land themselves, the mass of the people became landless. The countryside was infested with poor labourers who earned a living by hiring themselves out by the day, month or season. Such men had no rights, no certainty of employment and no interest in the soil they worked. They were paid a pittance which barely kept them alive and fed on a soup made of oil, vinegar and water with bread floating on it. If they refused to work, or demanded higher wages, outsiders from Portugal or Galicia replaced them. If they tried to cultivate the large amounts of land left derelict by their masters they were driven off by the police, the army or the Civil Guard. In any village square at dawn during the short season they could be seen huddled in ragged groups, hoping to be picked by the landlord's steward. The lives of these *braceros*, or landless men, were hard and miserable. At most times up till the Civil War there were 2,500,000 of them.

Some provinces, Catalonia, the Levante, Valencia and Alicante for example, had no *latifundia*. One, Galicia, even suffered from the opposite problem, *minifundia* or farms which were too small to support a family properly. Nevertheless, at least the starving Galician peasants owned something. They were not tormented by the sight of a rich landowner owning more land than he needed whilst they starved. It was this obvious unfairness which made matters so serious in the *latifundia*. A bitter hatred developed between landowners and peasants, a hatred which often flared into violence. The first revolt of *braceros* occurred at Malaga in 1840. Since then terrible outrages have become common. In 1850, for example, an army of eight hundred peasants, demanding a fairer distribution of the land, captured a town called Loja. Government forces crushed this revolt, hanged six of the ringleaders and sent four hundred to work in Africa. One historian has described the problem as 'that cancer of Spanish society, the unwieldy, uneconomic estates of the great landowner'. In the tapestry of hate which caused the Civil War there was no stronger thread than this 'disease' of the *latifundia*.

The Anarchists

Narváez died in 1868, boasting on his death-bed that he had shot all his enemies! Immediately a Liberal army rebellion broke out, for many officers had grown tired of the way the Queen allowed priests to interfere in politics. Royal troops were defeated and Isabella fled abroad. The revolution then followed the usual Liberal pattern. Two generals, Prim and Serrano, promised votes for all, a free press and the abolition of all monastic orders. They were not Republicans, however, and invited an Italian prince, Amadeo I, to reign in place of Isabella. This unfortunate man was disliked by almost everybody and treated as a foreigner. After two years he resigned. For the first time in her history Spain became a republic.

Disorder had been increasing steadily since 1868. With the strong hand of Narváez gone hardly a day passed without news of outrages, a revolt at Cadiz, a fight in Jerez, a governor murdered in church, or some new attack by the Carlist bands. Under the Republic matters grew worse. Carlists, dismayed at the attack on the Church, declared open war. Separatists clamoured for independence. The Republic itself failed to find an efficient leader. Its first prime minister, Figueras, lasted four months. Then he wrote his resignation, sent it to the Spanish Cortes or Parliament and took a train to France. He was the most successful; others resigned after shorter periods! Some, like Pi y Margall wanted the Separatists to have their way. To him, one central government seemed wrong; he said, 'I will divide and subdivide power.' Unfortunately it soon became clear that the Spanish love of independence knew no limits. Provinces, towns, even villages seemed to wish to be independent! Málaga, Seville, Granada, Cordova and Cartagena were all taken over by armed workers. Towns which did not want self-government were bombarded by rebellious ships of the Spanish fleet. After only a year the First Republic collapsed, replaced by a monarchy represented by Alfonso XII but controlled by rich landowners.

What lay behind all this disorder? We have already seen

how contrary ideas of the Church, the Liberals and the Army led to trouble. Now we must look at the Anarchists, for it was their beliefs which split Spain during the First and Second Republics.

An Anarchist dislikes all government. In his ideal world nobody would give orders and the country would be an association of independent districts or societies. The founder of the movement, a Russian revolutionary Michael Bakunin, thought all governments were wrong. He dreamed of a world

Michael Bakunin.

in which nobody gave orders but men and women decided what to do freely and without compulsion. After years in prison his ideas grew into a bitter hatred of all who governed or owned anything. Once when travelling he saw some men burning a house. He jumped out of his coach and helped them without bothering to enquire why they were doing it. To him it was enough that they wished to destroy something.

Such a belief made the Anarchist unique. Other men joined political parties because they wished to help rule their country. Anarchists alone wanted to destroy the government and give no orders. Their beliefs were brought into Spain in October 1868 by an Italian, Giuseppi Fanelli. Unable to speak Spanish, he managed to convey his meaning to some Madrid printers by his waving arms, excited voice and flashing dark eyes. One man said, 'we could understand his expressive mimicry and follow his speech'; another could still remember the tone of Fanelli's voice twenty years afterwards. Yet in Madrid where

Durruti—a famous Anarchist leader in the Civil War.

conditions were not too bad, where men still worked in small craftsmen's shops under a master they met every day, the conviction that all government is wrong did not spread. It was precisely where conditions were worse, in factory towns and the countryside of the *latifundia*, that such a belief was accepted eagerly. In Barcelona's gaunt, airless textile mills, for instance, underfed men and women slaved for very little so that their masters could make fortunes. Those who demanded more pay were sacked and replaced by *braceros*. So one problem met another and the poverty of the countryside increased the misery of the towns. To such starving workers and peasants Anarchism came with the force of a new religion.

It appealed even more strongly because Bakunin, and another Anarchist writer, Proudhon, also hated Christianity. In those parts where Churchmen were very unpopular because of their friendship with the rich landowners, Proudhon's favourite slogans, 'Property is theft' and 'God is evil' were soon on many people's lips. Bakunin himself never visited Spain but his love of destruction infected a passionate people in a most terrible way. Worse still, violence and violent strikes in which the workers often did not wish to make an agreement with their employers became common. At Cordova in 1905, for example, they demanded a seven-and-a-half-hour rest during an eight-hour day precisely because they knew their employers could not agree! In this respect Anarchist trade unions differed from normal ones. Called Anarcho-Syndicalist from the French word for 'trade union', they were all amalgamated into the C.N.T., the Confederación Nacional del Trabajo, in 1911. We shall read more of them later.

Much of the disorder during the First Republic was caused by this destructive belief. Preached by wandering, unpaid men, put into practice by workers who refused strike pay because they preferred to suffer, it attracted fanatical loyalty. In their misery men and women turned to dreams. Here seemed an easy answer to the unfairness which surrounded them. At a blow their enemies would be crushed and a new world would be created. It had its moral side, too. Although Anarchists refused to be married in church, never baptized their children, never used the word 'God', they remained faithful to their wives, gave up vices, such as heavy drinking or gambling, and despised money. As early as 1869 a foreigner, wrote, 'Visiting Spain . . . I was present at several of the meetings of these Socialist clubs. [He meant Anarchist.] They generally took place in disused churches. From the pulpit the orators attacked everything that had once been exalted there: God, religion, priests, riches.'[1] The Church was about to pay a heavy price for becoming the friend of the rich.

[1] Quoted by Gerald Brenan in *Spanish Labyrinth*.

'Two infamous jokes'

Many Liberal, middle-class people were now frightened. Because their attempts to befriend the people had failed dismally, they decided to join the landowners and aristocrats. This decision marks another turning-point in Spanish history, another step nearer disaster. The few who preached the old beliefs in liberty and the brotherhood of man were ignored. Instead, from 1875 until 1917, a fake system of government was operated by the landowners. On paper it appeared to be a democratic one which gave the people free voting rights. Actually two parties, the Conservatives led at first by Canovas del Castillo and the Liberals led by Sagasta, took it in turns to rule the country. Election results were faked regularly by the *caciques* or political leaders in each district so that seventy seats were always won by the Opposition. Periodically the other party took over after 'winning' the election. At the beginning of the twentieth century one Spaniard described these Parliaments and the way they were elected as 'two infamous jokes'.

Such a system was in some ways worse than a dictatorship, for it made people distrust democracy and turn to violent anarchism as the only solution. Normal political groups, such as the Socialist Party, formed in Madrid in 1879, and led by Pablo Iglesias, found it difficult to gain recruits precisely because they believed in free elections. With the Socialists there was no question of converting thousands as if by the waving of a wand. Iglesias worked hard to explain the principles of Socialism, particularly its belief in nationalization and free state education, to ignorant workmen who often had to be taught to read at the same time. Where conditions were worst progress was almost impossible and men and women became Anarchists instead. Only in Madrid and Castile did Socialism spread slowly. Even so, it was not until more extreme leaders like Largo Caballero took over from Iglesias at the turn of the century and Socialists began to join in Anarchist strikes that recruits poured in. Then the Socialist trade union, the U.G.T., the Unión General de Trabajadores, became as powerful as the C.N.T. Everywhere people faced with extreme unfairness reacted extremely.

Consequently the seventy years before the Civil War were

Anarchists' attempt to kill King Alfonso on his wedding day, 1906.

terrible ones. In 1869, when Spain was seeking a new king, its leader, General Prim, after describing the disorder and killing going on at that time, had asked, 'Who is going to venture into such a country?' Soon afterwards he was shot dead. The same question could have been asked for the next forty years as government, police and trade union workers became increasingly murderous. In 1892, when an Italian Anarchist was executed for attempting to kill a general, one of his friends threw a bomb into a theatre, killing twenty people. Four years later a bomb was hurled at a religious procession in Barcelona. Who threw it has never been discovered. It may have been an Anarchist or a friend of the government pretending to be one. The police, however, seized the opportunity to arrest hundreds of Anarchists. At Montjuich prison men were slashed with knives, burnt all over, or had their toe- and finger-nails pulled out. In revenge an Anarchist killed the Prime Minister, Canovas. So the tale of violence and murder continued, particularly in Barcelona, whose fanatical population included criminals from many lands. Both sides employed gangs of killers, called *pistoleros*; both took a life for a life with mathematical exactness. As Spain entered the twentieth

23

'At Montjuich prison men were slashed with knives. . . .' An old photograph of the castle.

century, the bomb, the gun, and the torture chamber were the only argument which seemed to interest either side.

Rivera and the end of the Monarchy

The long rule of the landowners was ended by the army. Abroad it had met with nothing but disaster. In 1895 Cuba had revolted against Spanish rule. Three years later the United States intervened on the side of the Cubans. The result of such an attack by a more powerful country was a deathroll of 200,000, the loss of the Spanish fleet, and the seizure by the Americans of the last remnants of Spain's empire, Cuba and the Philippines. This was a shattering blow to Spanish pride. It increased the dislike of military service amongst the poor and started a hatred of war itself amongst many intelligent people. One famous Liberal politician, Costa, remarked, 'The sepulchre of the Cid ought to be doublelocked.' The Cid is Spain's national hero. What Costa meant was that his country should forget about military glory and give up expeditions of the O'Donnell type. Nevertheless the Moroccan war dragged on without any decision. Spanish soldiers fought bravely with equipment as out of date as ever. Even the Moors had better guns whilst some Spanish rifles could not be fired for any length of time without becoming overheated.

At home, however, officers had plenty of power, especially as the new King, Alfonso XIII, was interested in soldiering. Officers enjoyed many privileges. By law they paid only half taxes and were allowed to travel on trains at reduced fares. Above all, they were encouraged by their commanders to think that the army had the right to change the government of Spain when it wished. In 1906 two hundred officers attacked the buildings of a newspaper which had dared to criticize them. The Government did nothing. Eleven years later a crisis occurred. Many younger officers had never liked the land-owner Government. The bad state of the army, which according to some infantry officers was 'absolutely disorganized', seemed insulting to them. In a pronunciamiento they told the King that he must 'entrust the government to politicians capable of convening honest elections'. Nobody could stand against them and the false election system was swept away at last. A new time of hope seemed to have dawned for Spain. Yet two facts ruined the revolution. First, nobody attempted to divide the great estates which remained to plague the country-side with beggars. Second, when the people tried to show support for the army's reforms, the officers soon indicated which side they were on. In Barcelona a strike was crushed by the very men it was meant to support. As the bullets killed workers and the cavalry charged, it was clear that the old Spain, deeply divided between rich and poor, remained.

The country again fell into disorder. Between 1918 and 1923 Spain had twelve governments. One newly appointed Prime Minister remarked gloomily, 'We shall not last more than eight or ten days' and he was right! Finally, when General Primo de Rivera, Captain General of Catalonia, seized power with the help of the army, the King and many Barcelona factory-owners, one of the retiring government said thankfully, 'Now I have added a new patron saint to the calendar—Saint Miguel Primo de Rivera, who has delivered me from the nightmare of governing.'

Rivera was every inch a soldier. He brought the discipline of the barrack square into Spanish life, and at least gave Spain one Government for seven years. His main concern was to end the Moroccan war where a Spanish force had just been destroyed at Anual. This he managed to do in 1927 with the help of the French army. At home he gave Spain law and order, trying in his practical way to improve roads, irrigate the dry areas, re-equip railways, install an efficient telephone system and develop hydroelectric power. But he did not get on well with the King and he despised freedom. The Cortes and all

'Rivera was every inch a soldier.' The dictator in Morocco.

municipal councils were closed; the press could not print what it liked, political parties were banned. Only trade unions were allowed to carry on, mainly because Rivera valued the support of the Catalan workers. On the other hand, the peasant was ignored to please the landowners. Wheat and olives remained specially protected. Taxes still hit the peasant and the shopkeeper hardest, leaving the landowner free to pretend his profits were less than they really were. The age-old Spanish problems were the same in 1930, when Rivera fled abroad after losing the support of the army and the King, as they had been when he came to power.

Only one important institution did change. To Alfonso the

King Alfonso XIII.

first free municipal elections for seven years seemed to be a vote against him. He knew he had many supporters but, fearing a civil war, he left the country. Quietly and sadly he drove to Cartagena and boarded a Spanish warship which took him to France. No one recognized him when he landed in Marseilles in the early hours of the next morning. The last Bourbon King of Spain had returned to a Republican country which did not even know him.

In the Cortes chamber a curtain was placed across the alcove where the throne had stood. The leaders of the Second Republic did not wish to be reminded of such objects as they prepared to build a new, better Spain.

27

3 The Second Republic

Manuel Azana, President of the Republic. 'A good speaker, an idealist and a scholar. . . .'

Fascism and Communism

The world into which the Second Republic was born in 1931 was a particularly troubled one. Grave unemployment had been caused by factories producing more goods than could be sold, first in the United States and then in Europe. In most industrial countries the workless queued for free bread and soup whilst factories and shipyards stood empty and idle.

There was also an emptiness in men's minds as well as their stomachs. The First World War had led to the collapse of old kingdoms and the rejection of old ideas, leaving men puzzled as to what to do. In their confusion they turned in various directions. Socialists and Communists were certain that State ownership of the major industries would be a first step towards a better, fairer world order. The more violent of the two, the Communists, blamed the middle and upper classes for all working-class suffering. They looked eagerly towards Russia for guidance. Here a workers' dictatorship was producing a kind of society new in world history. Many men, not all of them Communists, were impressed; one man returned from a visit to Russia and said, 'I have seen the future and it works.'

The Fascists in Italy and Nazis in Germany held different views. Neither were interested in nationalization providing the capitalists obeyed them. Both were influenced by the writings of a nineteenth-century poet called Sorel. In his opinion, a country could only be improved by a group of 'superior' men taking over; a new aristocracy in fact. Such a belief in practice meant rule by one party, a dictatorship instead of democracy. It led also to any other ideas being treated as wrong. For instance, the Nazis regarded the 'superior' men as racially pure Germans. Other peoples, particularly Jews, were despised and blamed for Germany's defeat in the First World War. Italian Fascists looked to the old Roman Empire for their inspiration; their leader, Mussolini, longed to reconquer Africa. Each philosophy preached racial hate of one form or another, each thought of life as a physical struggle to be won by the warlike, each looked upon their leader as a sort of god.

Such dangerous beliefs were brought to Spain by two men, Gimenez Caballero and Onésimo Redondo who founded a Fascist group called J.O.N.S. A similar doctrine had been

José Antonio Primo de Rivera, the founder of the Falange.

suggested by José Antonio Rivera, son of the dictator, whose Falange Española party believed in one political party only with, as his constitution put it, 'no parliament of the familiar type' but substituted instead of 'racial purity' a devotion to the Roman Catholic religion. The two parts of this Spanish Fascist movement united in 1933. Their numbers were small; they had no members in the Cortes in 1936. But their aggressive attitude made them a menace out of all proportion to their numbers. Here were men as full of violent dreams as the Anarchists. Indeed, some Anarchists had also read Sorel. A small, dedicated group of 'superior' men and women existed inside their ranks, called the F.A.I., the Federación Anarquista Ibérica.

It is against this background of world unrest and conflicting ideals that the age-old Spanish battles were fought during the

Second Republic. Not surprisingly, its history was as stormy and violent as that of the First. For most of the years before the Civil War, a Liberal and Socialist Government struggled against Conservative (landowner), Catholic and Fascist opposition, hindered by Anarchists and Separatists. In 1934 a Conservative Government led by Lerroux won the election and tried to undo the work of the previous three years. Finally, all the more revolutionary parties, Republicans, Socialists and Communists, united in what was called the 'Popular Front' to win the election of 16 February 1936. This caused their enemies to fear the country would go Communist. Led by many army officers, they revolted on 18 July. So began the Civil War.

Old enemies and unsolved problems

What went wrong? Why did well-meaning Liberal politicians like Azaña, Quiroga, Barrio, fail so completely? Mainly because being reasonable men they were suspended over the gap that divided the rich and poor of Spain. They lived in the Liberal world of 1812 and 1820. In 1931 their moderate policies merely annoyed their enemies and made their friends impatient for more drastic reforms. Had these men been the violent Communist revolutionaries which some of the generals claimed they might still be ruling Spain.

Azaña, Prime Minister and then President, was typical of the Republic. A good speaker, an idealist and a scholar, he followed the old-fashioned Liberal policy of attacking the Church. There may have been some value in this in 1820; in 1931 there were far more urgent problems. Foolishly he allowed his real enemies to organize themselves after the sudden collapse of their type of government and the flight of the King. A government threatened by Fascists, the generals and the landowners, gave first importance to writing a Constitution which stopped government payment of priests, suspended religious education and even abolished the monastic orders in some cases. Their attitude was understandable. No greater opponent of Liberal ideas existed at that time than the Spanish Church; the 1927 Catechism for use in schools went so far as to suggest that anyone reading a Liberal newspaper might be damned eternally! The Republic was hardly established when an important churchman, Cardinal Segura, denounced it and was forced to leave the country. Abroad, many Catholic churches were in favour of Liberal reforms; even the Pope agreed to Segura's dismissal. At home the Spanish Church remained as isolated and intolerant in its opinions as ever.

However, though it might side with the Republic's enemies, it was not the real enemy. Since its defeat in the Carlist wars it had lost much of its political power. Furthermore, although it was hated in areas such as New Castile, where only 5 per cent of the population went to church in 1931, it was loved in Navarre and the Basque provinces where the priest was the friend of his parishioners. In addition, educated Catholics, who often wished to support the Republic, could not agree to policies which left thousands of children temporarily without teachers. Badly needing all the friends it could get, the Republic's attack on the Church merely made more enemies. By 1933 the C.E.D.A. (Catholic) Party led by Gil Robles was the strongest single group in the country. Later it turned against the Republic.

Spain's basic illness, the landless peasant in the *latifundia*, was tackled halfheartedly. Azaña had said, 'a revolution, in order to be successful, must change the economic basis of power'. In other words, there must be a fairer distribution of available land. The Agrarian Law of 1932, which arranged for all unworked property of fifty-six acres or more to be nationalized, applied only to Andalusia, Estremadura and part of Castile. The Socialist Caballero, then Minister of Labour, realized that this only touched the fringe of the problem. He described it as 'an aspirin to cure an appendicitis'. Even this small dose of 'medicine' was administered slowly or not at all, possibly because there was not enough money to pay for such reforms and modernization. Naturally, the peasants grew impatient. One wrote, 'Time is passing and the land remains in the hands of the *caciques*.' By 1934 only 12,260 peasants had received any land. The other two-and-a-half million must have wondered how many years would pass before they were lucky. Then came the Conservative Government of Lerroux which reduced the slightly increased wages of the labourer, and stopped all nationalization. With some men reduced to working for food only, José Antonio de Rivera, founder of the

Falange, declared, 'Life in the Spanish countryside is absolutely intolerable.'

The glorious new age certainly did not dawn in the countryside. When the Liberals returned with their Popular Front government in 1936 many peasants, infuriated by their conditions, marched into the empty areas owned by their masters, without waiting for new laws. From 1931 terrible events had occurred which reminded old men of the worst riots of the previous century. At Castilblanco in Estremadura, furious *braceros* killed four Civil Guards, smashed their heads in and gouged their eyes out. At Casas Viejas Anarchists revolted and besieged the Civil Guard bàrracks. Reinforcements hurried from Cadiz, set fire to the villagers' cottages and shot many men and boys in the smoking ruins.

Separatism and army plots

If the Republican politicians failed to solve the real problem they also ignored the real danger. The story of the previous hundred years showed clearly that this was the army. Azaña failed to understand this. Instead of forming a new people's army, he referred to such a danger as a 'myth' although a secret army society, the U.M.E., Unión Militar Española, already existed to plan a revolt. He encouraged army officers to resign during a drastic reorganization of the armed forces. Since they were given full pay many did so, some because they were Liberals who disliked army life, some in order to plot in peace and quiet. Those officers who remained were the true professionals, every one of them likely to be against Liberal ideas. Azaña said he was not interested in a soldier's politics and appointed General Goded as Chief of Staff. This man was very political indeed!.He hated the Government and made no secret of it; he had even rebelled once against Primo de Rivera. When, in August 1932, General Sanjurjo started a revolt in Seville, Azaña's Government knew of it beforehand and it was crushed. Instead of taking this as a warning, the Prime Minister felt confident that all rebellions would be as easy to handle. Nothing seemed able to alter his belief that he could rule a disorderly and divided country without an army to support him. Meanwhile the military plotters continued with their plans. In the north the Carlist *requetés*, or volunteers, drilled openly whilst their officers were trained in an unofficial military academy at Pamplona!

The disasters which were to come from ignoring their enemies were equalled by those which came from trying to please their friends. The Basques, Catalans and others were really interested in regional independence. This was almost the only reason why they supported the Republic. Forgetting what had happened in 1874, the Republicans inserted a clause in their Constitution which said any region could have self-government if it wished. To say this in Spain was like taking all the nuts and bolts out of an engine. Spain, like the engine, began to fall to pieces in a way which pleased the Separatists and Anarchists but infuriated the army officers who believed in a united country. For example, when in 1932 Catalonia was given a Charter of Autonomy allowing it to have a separate president and parliament, its own language and flag, the Basques demanded the same privilege. So did other parts of Spain. When Lerroux's Government refused such demands a serious Communist revolt occurred amongst the miners of Asturias which needed tanks, troops and aeroplanes to put down. Simultaneously Catalan politicians, encouraged in their separatism by the Government's attitude, proclaimed their complete independence. As a result Catalonia was conquered by Republican troops. Later the Popular Front Government restored the Charter to the Catalans. Such change of policy, such violence, did not help men to feel confidence in the Government.

Above all, the Republic, attacked by both its enemies and its friends, failed to keep order. The country was plagued by violence and disobedience of every sort. Anarchists burned churches, Socialists went on strike, Fascists toured the streets in fast cars killing their opponents. Meetings of the Cortes were a continual riot with members being searched for weapons as they entered. The papers were full of details of murders and strikes, strikes just finished, strikes just starting, strikes threatened, sympathetic strikes, sit-down strikes and general strikes. Each section of Spain continued its private war with those it hated whilst the Government looked on helplessly. A few days before the Civil War began, Gil Robles said that 160 churches had been destroyed, and 269 priests

A burned church, 1936.

murdered in four months. These dreadful figures may have been an exaggeration but no one seemed surprised or felt like contradicting him. He concluded his speech with these words: 'A country can live under a monarchy or a republic, with a parliamentary or a presidential system, under Communism or Fascism. But it cannot live in anarchy . . . we are today present at the funeral service of a democracy.' The man who said this was just as much to blame as everybody else, for there were many who caused violence in order to complain about it afterwards. Yet he was right. The army conspirators realized that the time was ripe for action.

The murder of Sotelo

The chief conspirator in the Carlist north was Emilio Mola. This scholarly-looking, crafty man was no reckless Sanjurjo, ready to burst into half prepared revolt. Methodically he made his plans. Persuasively he rallied supporters to his cause. Although military and civilian conspirators had been alerted in every town, the tricky task of assembling the leading generals at the right time and in the right place required much thought. Franco was needed in Africa to take command of the Legion. Somehow he must escape from the Canary Islands, where he had been sent by a Government which distrusted him. Goded, far away in the Balearic Islands, needed to arrive in Barcelona. Sanjurjo, chosen to lead the revolt, must fly in from Portugal where he had lived since the 1932 rising. People whose aims were not really the same had to be persuaded to work together, Carlists with Falangists, Monarchists with disappointed Liberals. As far as possible nothing was to be left to chance. Even so, Mola feared what might happen if the Socialist and Anarchist workers stopped quarrelling amongst themselves and stood firm. Then the swift seizure of power which was planned might fail, a long war might follow. 'It will be borne in mind', he wrote, 'that the action, in order to crush as soon as possible a strong and well-organized enemy, will have to be very violent.'

The original date for the revolt was April 1936. Many factors caused this to be altered. General del Barrio, a key man, became frightened and refused to act. General Franco still debated whether to join the conspirators at all. The Carlists wanted a guarantee that the monarchy would be re-established on their terms. Mola could not give this because many of the future rebels were Republicans who did not want a King. The heat of a Spanish July had arrived before all their difficulties were overcome. By then the danger of some form of workers' dictatorship seemed too great for any more arguments or delays. The new *Reconquista* must come first. On 9 July many leaders of the rebellion assembled in Pamplona to watch the annual festival during which wild bulls are released in the streets for young men to fight. All knew that something far more violent than wild bulls was about to be loosed upon Spain.

Appropriately, the signal for revolt was a dreadful murder. On 12 July, Lt. José Castillo, a member of the Republican Assault Guards, was shot dead in Madrid. His furious comrades decided upon a terrible deed for which they had no official permission. At about three o'clock on the morning of 13 July two lorry-loads of Guards went to the home of Calvo

'All knew that something far more violent than wild bulls was about to be loosed upon Spain.' Festival of St. Fermin, Pamplona.

Sotelo, an enemy of the Republic who was leader of the Opposition parties in the Cortes. The sleepy and astonished man was ordered to come to police headquarters for questioning. He tried to telephone the police to see if they were speaking the truth. He got no reply because the phone was out of order.

This was suspicious. However, Captain Condés, the leader of the group, assured him they were on official business. Sotelo's wife was worried because only a few days before her husband's life had been threatened. She hurriedly packed him a few personal belongings. He went and kissed his sleeping children goodbye. Then he reassured her and said, half joking, that he would be all right, 'unless these gentlemen are going to blow out my brains'. She last saw him take his seat in the truck, wave and disappear at high speed. After only a few moments a gunman seated behind, leaned forward and fired two shots into his neck so fast that those in the truck thought he had fired only once. It was midday before anybody realized that the bloodstained body left in the city mortuary was that of a leading politician.

The revolt would have started whether Sotelo had died or

not. But a death which could be blamed upon the Government was of great propaganda value to the generals. Five days later Franco was in Tetuan and the Civil War had begun. On that hot July day, with Madrid radio blaring contradictory news and rifle fire crackling in town and village, Spaniards must have asked themselves whether this was just another officers' revolt or whether something far more terrible was about to happen. The cunning Mola, the grimly efficient Franco, must have wondered too, as they studied their maps, organized air transport and equipment, appealed to Germany and Italy for help and issued orders which were to lead to Spain's greatest disaster.

4 Rebellion and Revolution

Franco is proclaimed Head of the Spanish State, October 1936.

Francisco Franco

On 20 July 1936 General Sanjurjo boarded a private plane at Lisbon. He carried far too much luggage and so the pilot, Ansaldo, asked if two cases could be left behind. Both contained uniforms the old soldier intended to wear as ruler of Spain. He refused and forced the pilot to take off with a dangerously overloaded aircraft. As it nosed painfully upwards, Ansaldo fought desperately to clear some trees. There was a jarring crack as his propeller struck some branches. Gently, like a wounded bird, the plane settled on a wall. A mighty roar and a sheet of flame followed as the reserve petrol tank exploded. Ansaldo struggled to help Sanjurjo, who sat as if paralysed with almost a smile on his face, but the smoke and fire forced him back. Reluctantly he crawled to safety. A few moments later nothing was left except blackened wreckage and the white bones of the general. Because of this strange accident Francisco Paulino Hermenegildo Teódulo Franco, a Galician from the sea port of El Ferrol, was given the title 'Generalissimo of all the Armed Forces and Head of the Government of the Spanish State'. He has held this position ever since.

This soldier had really wanted to be a sailor like his father and elder brother. The house in which he was born on 4 December 1892, a three-storied one with balconies overlooking the street, stands in a town which has bred many fine seamen. Atlantic gales blow into the long 'ria', or bay, on which it stands. Its children play by the water's edge or gaze enviously at the ships which come and go. Little Francisco was no exception. As a boy he played pirates on the gang-planks of ferry-steamers and fished with a homemade rod and line. The sea called him to adventure. Unfortunately when the time came for him to join the navy Spain was cutting down her fleet. At fourteen years of age, as 'a slender youth of delicate features and large shining eyes', to quote a friend's description, he went to the Infantry Academy at the Alcázar fortress in Toledo instead. On 13 July 1910 he became a Second Lieutenant in the Spanish army. Two years later he landed in Morocco to fight the Moors.

Like many Spanish officers, he spent all his young manhood fighting a cruel enemy. The Riffs were fierce fighters who tortured their prisoners. Life on campaign was dangerous and short. Sixty-five per cent of the army suffered from malaria. In one battle, only one in ten of the officers of Franco's regiment survived. Despite such dangers, the young Galician rose swiftly because of his hard work and bravery. He was successively the youngest Captain, Major, Colonel and General in the Spanish army. On the battlefield he was very lucky. Once his horse was shot from under him, often his cap and cloak were riddled with bullets. At Bruit in 1916 he was so severely wounded in the stomach that according to a friend 'he hovered between life and death but his youth pulled him through'. Years later he was buried by a shell explosion.

Such adventures made him a stern, ruthless man. When made director of the Military Academy at Saragossa in 1928 he told the young cadets that a soldier's life was not the road 'to pleasure and delight'; 'it involved', he said, 'great sufferings, hardships and sacrifices', although he finished by saying, 'it must not be forgotten that he who suffers conquers'. This was the hard belief that years of warfare had taught General Franco. This was the attitude to life of the man who led the rebels in the Civil War.

There is, of course, more to him than bravery and a strong sense of duty. Other generals, Sanjurjo and Rivera for instance, were equally brave. Few worked as hard or waited as patiently. The landing at Alhucemas Bay in 1927, which trapped the Moorish army and ended the Moroccan war, was planned by Franco. An army was brought ashore on a coast defended by 10,000 Moors with only trifling losses. This patience and careful planning applied to his private life also. When he fell in love with Carmen Polo Martinez-Valdés her parents objected because he was only a lieutenant. 'I will come back as a Colonel and ask you again', he said. He did, and both Carmen and her parents said 'yes'! Most Spaniards are quick and impulsive. Sometimes Franco will think about a problem for years before acting. He did not join the 1932 revolt and some Monarchists suspected with good reason that he was a Republican. The conspirators in the July revolt were not sure until early 1936 that he would be with them.

Yet there could be no doubt about which side he was on in a divided Spain. His love of military discipline and unity made him hate the Anarchists, with their dreams of no government at all, and the Separatists who wished to divide Spain. The working-class societies of the Socialists and Communists were equally detested by this child of the middle classes. By nature and training he is a dictator, accustomed to being obeyed. 'A century and a half of parliamentary democracy', he said later, 'accompanied by the loss of immense territory, three civil wars, and the imminent danger of national disintegration add up to a disastrous balance sheet, sufficient to discredit the parliamentary system in the eyes of the Spanish people.' Many would disagree, for Spain had no truly democratic system whilst some of these disasters occurred. Yet this is how

Franco feels about democracy. In a disorganized country, full of passionate idealists and dreamers, he believes in unity, discipline and no 'luxuries' like personal freedom.

In 1923 the Government had made a decision which was of great importance in the war just starting. Franco was appointed commander of the Spanish Foreign Legion. This regiment had been founded in 1920 by Millán-Astray, a strange, fierce man who had lost an arm, eye and leg in battle.

General Millán-Astray with Franco.

In spite of its name, it consisted mostly of Spaniards who served for five years overseas. From the start its founder was determined that the Legion should be a privileged, expert army. The men who formed its *banderas*, or battalions, received twice as much pay as ordinary soldiers and were referred to as 'Gentlemen Legionaries'. At the same time they were harshly disciplined and death was the punishment for disobedience. In battle they soon proved themselves Spain's finest troops who stormed forward singing their song 'Death the bride'. Franco led them with a courage which they did not forget in the years ahead. In a special way, they and the Moorish troops attached to them became his own army.

In 1934 the Communist miners of Asturias revolted. Spain's leaders were afraid to use ordinary troops against such skilled dynamiters. 'I decided', wrote the War Minister later, 'to call on units which Spain maintains for her defence, whose *métier* is to fight and die in the accomplishment of their duty.' He sent for the Legion and asked their old commander, Franco, to direct them. After fifteen days of fighting the legionaries defeated the miners, occupying the chief towns of Oviedo and Gijón. They then behaved as if they were in Morocco. Hundreds of miners were tortured or shot after capture. Thus Spain had its first experience of the Foreign Legion. In the war now beginning they were to have much more.

The rising begins

On 17 July 1936, the day Captain Bebb arrived in Las Palmas with his pretty 'tourists', the first military rising started at Melilla in Morocco. Two Colonels, Gazapo and Seguí, decided to seize all important buildings in the town. Their commander, Romerales, found out from a traitor and sent a lieutenant to arrest them. Trapped in the map department of the headquarters, Gazapo telephoned to the Foreign Legion for help after persuading the lieutenant to surrender. Some minutes later Seguí forced Romerales to resign at revolver point. Many officers of the garrison wondered what to do. Should they join their rebellious comrades? Or should they remain loyal and so avoid another failure like Sanjurjo's in 1932? Some merely surrendered: others contacted Madrid for instructions or help. Meanwhile the more determined rebel officers captured most of the town's public buildings, including the Socialist headquarters. The Socialists fought back and a fierce battle raged throughout Melilla's poorer districts. By evening, however, the town had fallen to Franco's men.

Mola had said they should be 'very violent'. The rebels celebrated this, their first success of the war, by shooting all leading Republicans, Socialists and freemasons like General Romerales. Their actions, like that of the legion in Asturias in 1934, were a grim taste of what was to come. In every town captured during the next three years, the crackle of rifle fire, the bloodstained and bullet-scarred walls against which men died, were to indicate a new *Reconquista*. Spain's army leaders believed in ridding the country of Communists as surely as the warriors of old had killed Moors. One general, Queipo de Llano, expressed the feelings of some of his friends when he was told that half Spain was Communist. 'Half Spain?' he remarked, 'Very well. We shall exterminate half Spain.' In other Moroccan towns, Tetuan, Ceuta and Larache, there were similar successful risings that day and the next. All saw swift and ruthless executions.

With Morocco secure the rebels' signal, *Sin novedad* which means 'as usual', was passed to the mainland on 18 July. Republican leaders were taken by surprise. Their officials telephoned town after town to discover what was happening. At the same time Government spokesmen tried to reassure the people. On 17 July, after a frantic phone call from Romerales, the Prime Minister, Casares Quiroga, announced publicly, 'A section of the army, disloyal to its oath, has taken up arms and risen against the State. . . . The rebels are localized groups. The nation under arms is joining forces with the loyal troops in defence of the Republic.' During that night he phoned Las Palmas to get in touch with Franco. He was told he was away inspecting troops: actually he was dictating his famous manifesto and preparing to fly to Tetuan.

All night people filled the streets and cafés of Madrid asking for news. As Cadiz, Seville, Jerez, Algeciras, La Linea and Cordoba fell to the rebels, the Government announced, 'No one, absolutely no one on the Spanish mainland has taken part in this plot.' Working people were not impressed by such statements. Large, excited crowds surrounded government buildings demanding weapons to defend the Republic. Quiroga refused, hoping that enough of the army would remain loyal to make this unnecessary. Such hopes were not fulfilled. On that tragic day, too many telephone calls were

Quiroga, whose phone calls were answered by the wrong people.

being answered by the wrong people. Instead of the civil governor of the town, a rebel voice would shout *Arriba España*. Those governors who were still in control were told to refuse the workers weapons. As a result many were killed by the rebels.

Most surprising were the events in Seville. Queipo de Llano drove into the city with four officers and calmly arrested its military commander. Then he hurried round to the infantry barracks where most of the troops happened to be on parade. Queipo congratulated their Colonel on having decided to rebel. When told that he had not, he ordered this soldier back to his own office for a talk. Once inside he shouted, 'You are my prisoner', and arrested him and his officers. Later the artillery regiments decided to join Queipo and when the Governor found himself surrounded by troops he too surrendered. By

Queipo de Llano surrounded by an admiring crowd.

mid-afternoon the enterprising general had almost succeeded in capturing a city of 250,000 people singlehanded! But his cheek failed to bluff the workers. Barricades were hastily built and eleven churches and a silk mill burned down. As the Seville darkness was lit up by flames and disturbed by the noise of battle, Madrid radio announced, 'Complete calm prevails throughout the peninsula.'

Spain divides

That night in Madrid the Liberal Quiroga resigned and a new Government led by Professor José Giral decided to arm the trade unionists. This decision was necessary if the Republic was to survive. Everywhere, it seemed, the men with weapons, the Falangists, the Carlists, the Civil Guard, police and army, had rebelled. Only the trade unionists were prepared to fight for the 'Popular Front' Government. All that day Madrilenos had chanted, 'Arms, arms, arms'. Taxi drivers had offered vehicles to help fight the rebels. The U.G.T. had already armed its young men with 8,000 rifles. Quiroga had hesitated because he feared a Communist-type revolution. His successors decided on the only act likely to stop a swift victory by the generals.

At dawn on 19 July lorries loaded with arms rumbled through the Madrid streets carrying rifles and machine-guns to the C.N.T. and U.G.T. offices. In many towns of Spain similar events took place. With cries of 'They shall not pass' the workers armed themselves. Their determination and ruthlessness equalled that of the generals. They, too, would fight a *reconquista*. They, too, would free their beloved country, only this time from the hated landowners, factory bosses, churchmen and army officers. Murders and executions grew more frequent in towns still held by the Republic. At sea many navy crews mutinied and shot their officers in order to prevent a revolt. The pent-up hatred of generations burst out on that dreadful day as all over Spain people settled their differences.

Wild confusion reigned, as towns joined one side or the other. In Barcelona a battle flared up between Anarchists and soldiers. Rebel troops were overpowered by men and women who captured machine-gun positions with their bare hands, helped by sections of the Civil Guard which here alone remained loyal to the Government. In Communist Asturias Colonel Aranda seized the town of Oviedo by trickery only to be besieged by furious miners. At San Sebastian, also, matters did not go well for the conspirators who found themselves trapped in clubs and hotels. Franco's own Galician countryside saw fighting and El Ferrol fell to the rebels although bombarded by Republican warships.

The Carlist areas, Burgos, Saragossa, Pamplona and Valladolid, did not need to be captured. Eagerly but with quiet dignity they joined Mola. So did Old Castile, Segovia and Ávila, where one of the founders of Spanish Fascism, Onésimo Redondo, was released from prison. He was luckier than José Antonio de Rivera. Confined in a Republican gaol at Alicante, he was shot in November. Estremadura and most of Cáceres province fell to the rebels although Badajoz remained loyal. Andalusia stood little chance after the arrival of

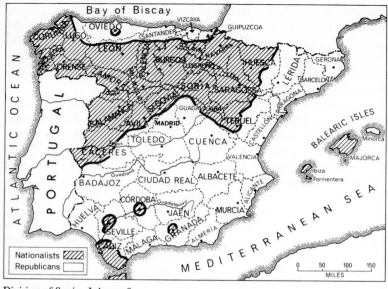

Division of Spain, July 1936.

Franco's Army of Africa. Neither did Seville, where the legionaries gave de Llano control at last. Amidst the chaos a great deal depended upon what happened in Madrid. By the evening of the 19th rebel officers, led by General Fanjul, had decided to act. Next day the first important battle of the war was fought in Spain's capital.

Battle for the Montana Barracks

Fanjul arrived at the Montana barracks, a large building set on a hill in the centre of Madrid, during the afternoon. He then wasted time making speeches and declaring martial law. His officers, many of them young Fascists, must have realized the difficulties they faced. In Madrid, the birthplace of Spanish Socialism, enthusiastic workers were armed and ready. Thousands of people carried rifles. The Assault Guards and militia were loyal to the Republic. No amount of bluff could capture such a stronghold; no sudden seizure of a headquarters building at revolver point would help here. Sure enough, when the rebels attempted a march through the streets they were confronted by an immovable crowd of people, singing and shouting defiance. They retired to the barracks to crouch by their machine-guns. Many must have wondered how long ammunition would last, how long the thick walls surrounding them could hold off the impatient Madrileños. Other Madrid garrisons which had rebelled were as isolated and surrounded as themselves. Outside help was their only hope but Franco and Mola were far away.

Night fell, a hot summer night illuminated by burning churches. Black smoke formed artificial clouds in a red sky. A smell of burning timber pervaded the air. The dome of St Nicholas's Church appeared like a helmet of sparks and flames. Hot lead oozed from it. Eventually, like Spain itself at that moment, it split open and crumbled away in ruins. A feeling of excitement and suspense filled the city as occasional machine-gun fire stuttered from the Montana area.

With dawn, preparations for an attack began. It was as if the entire population was on the move. From houses and tenements, from side streets and squares, people converged on the barracks shouting 'Death to Fascism' and 'All aid to the Republic'. Moving slowly forward, almost lost in the crowds, were three armoured cars and a beer lorry dragging guns. The guns rolled crazily over the cobbles, crushing many feet. Soon thousands of riflemen were in position behind trees or barricades. Overhead Republican aircraft dropped leaflets on the rebels, ordering them to surrender. Loudspeakers made the same demand. When no white flag appeared on the massive building, the assault was ordered.

The open spaces around the barracks became a battlefield. Bullets whined across squares and boulevards, tearing bark from trees, splintering stonework, killing or wounding men. Now and again a gun was fired. Republican aircraft dived upon the stronghold and released bombs. Smoke and flames added to the uproar. After five hours of battle a white flag appeared at one of the narrow windows. Fanjul had been wounded and some of his men wished to surrender. With shouts of joy militiamen left their cover to run forward. As they did so a stream of bullets laid them silent or screaming on the ground. This treachery, probably the result of disorder within the fortress, happened twice. It increased the crowd's fury and sealed the fate of the defenders.

3*

Just before midday the fiery Madrileños could no longer be held back by experienced Assault Guards who realized they need only wait for the inevitable surrender. Yelling 'Onward' and 'To the struggle', or singing the stirring old Republican *Hymn to Riego*, the mob moved into the hail of machine-gun fire, leaping over the bodies of their comrades who often lay writhing and slithering in their own blood. Flying bullets swept the square, mowing down the first lines. Those behind, often completely unarmed, were in little danger. By sheer weight of numbers they conquered. One eyewitness described how 'a huge solid mass of bodies like a ram' hit the door and burst it open.

As workers rushed into the building, the tiny figures guarding the windows vanished. A short, unearthly silence was broken by a mighty cheer from those outside as a solitary militiaman appeared framed in a window, waving and throwing boxes of rifles to the crowd. Then the scream of dying soldiers began to echo through stone corridors and galleries. One giant man was seen to be throwing not ammunition boxes, but officers down to those below. They fell like rag dolls, their legs threshing, their bodies writhing. An officer zigzagged along an open balcony, trying to dodge his pursuers. He was tripped and spiralled into the crowd, who trampled him to pulp. When nearly all his men were dead the wounded Fanjul was led away for trial and execution. Those rebels still free in the city fled north to join Mola. Dusk fell on a square littered with the debris of war, bodies, clothing, empty ammunition boxes. Darkness hid the blood from view. At almost the same hour Barcelona's fighting ended in a similar way with the storming of the Atarazanas barracks by Anarchists. Both great cities had been saved for the Republic.

There was now no hope of quick victory for the generals. From half-way up the Portuguese frontier a line could be drawn across Spain, running north-west to the Guadarrama mountains, down to Teruel and north to the Pyrenees. To the north and west except for a coastal strip held by the Basques, the rebels, or Nationalists, were in control. The south and east remained loyal to the Republic. A divided country had been split geographically.

Spanish bloodbath

Although cut in two by conquest, Spain was really disunited in every town and province. Each had its Socialists and Falangists, its Catholics and Liberals, its landowners and *braceros*. Consequently behind the front line both sides decided to destroy their enemies in case they rebelled. This combination of fear and hatred led to thousands of deaths and appalling cruelty.

In Nationalist Spain all Socialists and Communists, all freemasons and trade unionists, were arrested. Many were shot. A month after the rebellion began the Count of Vallellano was driving near Aranda. 'That's Red Aranda,' he said to his companion, a Red Cross representative, 'I am afraid we had to put the whole town in prison and execute very many people.' On the island of Majorca Falangist gangs scoured the fields and villages, taking men straight from their work to be shot. Often the victims' meals were left uneaten on the table or their wives hurried into the house too late to catch a last glimpse of their husbands. Altogether 3,000 were executed in seven months. Terrorized doctors certified that such people had 'died of cerebral congestion'. At first bodies both here and in Spain were left in the open to frighten people into submission. Later they were cleared away, especially in northern Spain after General Mola announced that he was inconvenienced by the number of corpses at the roadside! The killings themselves became less public. Rifle fire would ring out from some remote spot, from an orchard, or a hillside shielded by trees.

In Republican Spain the murders were worse because disorder encouraged men to take the law into their own hands. Century-old hatreds caused horrible actions. Militia gangs with no authority from the Government, gangs with names like 'Red Lions', 'Furies' or 'Spartacus', moved about burning churches and killing priests. Between July and September 1936 75,000 people were killed by such terrorists. Compared with the cold-blooded and methodical Nationalist executions, some Republicans behaved like wild beasts. When the time came to shoot rebel leaders at Barcelona an official firing squad was helped by crowds of spectators who suddenly joined in. An eyewitness wrote, 'Everyone seemed to be shooting at the four officers. And when the shooting was over, the condemned men could no longer be recognized, they were shot to pieces, and it was almost impossible to put their bodies, which now possessed the consistency of a liquid, into the waiting coffins.'[1]

Churchmen were particularly unlucky, and some paid with their lives for having deserted the poor. One bishop was killed in front of a laughing crowd. Two others were forced to wash the decks of a prison ship before being shot at Málaga. Several priests were burned alive. Even women were not safe. A nun who refused to marry a militiaman was executed. The mother of a Jesuit was choked to death with a crucifix. Some sensitive people went mad at the horrors they witnessed. Yet one priest at least realized how the Church had failed and said, 'The Reds have destroyed our churches, but we had first destroyed the Church.' By contrast, Basque priests were unharmed because they were friends of the poor.

Such cruelty went side by side with pride and honesty. Anarchists refused to steal any of the precious objects in the churches they burnt. In August an American visited the cruiser, *Miguel de Cervantes*, where the men had shot their officers. The rooms of the dead men were locked up; their property untouched. He was shown the Admiral's cabin. There was no disorder. Everything was as he had left it. Only his chair, riddled with bullet holes, its cushion sticky with blood, told what had happened. 'We may have to kill to create a better Spain', the men seemed to be saying, 'but we will not imitate the rich and become thieves.'

And so with blood, pain, hatred and high ideals, with one side roaring revolutionary songs and the other chanting Carlist and Falangist hymns, the civil war began.

The revolution begins

The generals claimed they had rebelled to prevent a workers' revolution and this is exactly what happened in those areas still controlled by the Republic. In Madrid the Socialist U.G.T. was the real power, not the Government. Huge portraits of Lenin, the founder of Communist Russia, were fixed

[1] From unpublished memoir of Jaume Miravitlles quoted in *Civil War in Spain*, ed. R. Payne, Secker and Warburg.

up beside those of Largo Caballero, the Socialist leader. In Barcelona the Anarchist C.N.T., led by gunmen like Durruti and García Oliver, decided to forget its principles and to join forces with Luis Companys, the Catalan President. An 'Anti-Fascist Militia Committee' made up of Anarchists, Socialists and Communists, took charge of the city. All over Republican Spain similar events occurred. The middle-class Liberal Azaña was still officially President of Spain. Few took any notice of him. His dream of a normal democracy had been destroyed by extremists on either side.

The excitement, the feeling that dreams were at last coming true, was most intense among the industrial workers of Barcelona. On 5 August 1936 Franz Borkenau visited the city. The crowds who thronged the Ramblas, a wide central street very popular for afternoon walks, looked different from any he had seen before. Most men were dressed in working-clothes, overalls, caps and so on. Nobody wore hats because Barcelona radio had warned people this was a middle-class habit! Another observer noticed this and wrote, 'Today there is not a hat, a collar or a tie to be seen.' Nearly every man carried a rifle, many walking with girl-friends or wives on one arm and a weapon on their shoulder. Expensive cars, confiscated by the unions, roared along the streets, decorated with union initials in white paint, F.A.I., U.G.T., C.N.T., P.S.U.C. (the Socialist party of Catalonia), and P.O.U.M., the Communist union which did not take orders from Russia. Borkenau saw one or two cars which displayed all these initials, possibly to

'Somehow an army had to be formed. . . .' Militiamen training near Madrid.

show how loyal they were! Most factories had been taken over by workers; all churches closed or burned. Church law was forgotten also. Marriages took place without a religious ceremony, an unheard-of thing in Catholic Spain.

This situation continued for some months. George Orwell, the English writer, arrived to fight for the Republic in December. Of Barcelona he wrote: 'It was the first time that I had ever been in a town where the working class was in the saddle. Practically every building of any size had been seized by the workers and was draped with red flags or with the red and black flags of the Anarchists; every wall was scrawled with the hammer and sickle and with the initials of the revolutionary parties; almost every church had been gutted and its images burnt. . . . Every shop and café had an inscription saying it had been collectivized; even the bootblacks had their boxes painted red and black. Waiters and shopwalkers looked you in the face and treated you as an equal. . . . Tipping was forbidden by law.' The wishes of the Anarchists, Communists and Socialists seemed to have come true overnight. In the first thrill of success few stopped to think how different were these beliefs. Obviously the city could become Anarchist, Socialist or Communist but not all three at once!

Even so, the appearance of a complete revolution was deceptive. Although most of the poor were in favour of the changes many of the rich merely pretended to be revolutionaries to save themselves from imprisonment or death. Orwell realized this and wrote, 'Great numbers of well-to-do bourgeois [middle-class] were simply lying low and disguising themselves as proletarians [workers] for the time being.'

Madrid in August 1936 had a less revolutionary air about it. Clearly it was a city at war. All the younger men seemed to be wearing militia uniform. But hardly any carried rifles, and there were still plenty of well-dressed men and luxurious cars about. A sign of the old ways, begging children, could be seen alongside something very new, young girls walking in the street without male escorts. Yet it was too revolutionary for one horrified conservative. She wrote: 'The appearance of Madrid was incredible; the bourgeoisie giving the clenched salute. . . . Even beauty parlours and barber's shops had been nationalized and their owners given jobs with their former assistants.' The Anarchist countryside would have horrified her even more. The few unburned churches had been turned into garages or storehouses. Some villages had actually abolished money. Of one, an Anarchist wrote, 'Here in Fraga you can throw banknotes into the street and no one will take any notice.'

Whether visible or not, whether halfhearted or enthusiastic, there was no doubt a revolution had taken place. From the moment the Republican Government found it had been deserted by most of its army and police and decided to arm the people it really gave control to what Salvador de Madariaga, a Spanish Liberal, described as 'that ill-assorted, loose group of tribes known as the U.G.T., the C.N.T., the F.A.I., the P.O.U.M., the P.U.S.C., the Communist Party. . . .' And he added, 'The very aim of these tribes was not, as might have been thought, to win the war against the Rebels. For most of the time it was to achieve a proletarian revolution, though not the same, for each tribe had a revolution of its own to achieve.'

Meanwhile Mola advanced with the Carlist *requetés* from the north, and Franco arranged for his Foreign Legion to be transported across the Straits of Gibraltar. The Republican leaders counted up the number of officers who had remained loyal. They discovered that of 525, only 25 had ever been properly trained at a military college! A strange, unequal contest seemed about to begin.

The legion advances

Amidst the confusion and slaughter of the first days of the war two men kept their heads. Although far apart, generals Mola and Franco did not allow themselves to be disheartened by failures in Madrid and Barcelona. Whatever their feelings, both had to concentrate upon the military problem facing them. This was to join forces as soon as possible and take Spain's capital.

To do this Franco had to get his troops across the Straits, a narrow stretch of water guarded by Republican naval units consisting of the battleship *Jaime Primero*, three cruisers, sixteen destroyers and some submarines. It should have been difficult. In fact, the killing of all their officers meant that these warships were controlled by seamen unable to operate them properly.

Most just managed to wander back to Cartagena where they did little for the rest of the war. Franco's first troops were flown to Spain in German Junkers aircraft; the remainder crossed in merchant ships protected by Italian fighters. By 6 August the lift was complete and Franco himself flew from Tetuan to Seville. Without delay, he made his plans. The best route to

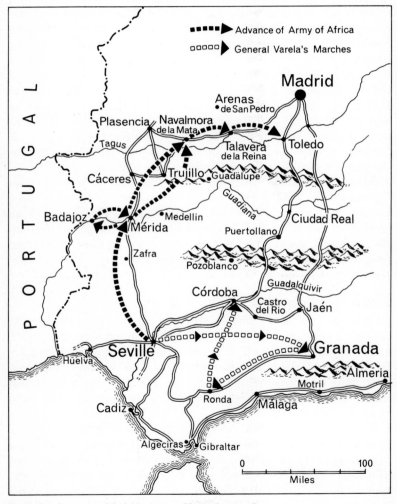

Franco's advance on Madrid, August–November 1936.

meet Mola and take Madrid was by road to Badajoz, so that the frontier with Portugal would be closed to the Republic, then up the Tagus river valley to the capital. An alternative, the railway line through the Sierra Morena mountains, was held by Republican forces.

Yagüe, a Falangist, was chosen to lead the advance. In detachments of a hundred, his men raced up the middle of the dusty roads in convoys of lorries. If a town seemed to be in the hands of the militia, they would halt, wait for their artillery to arrive, bombard the defences and attack. At Mérida Yagüe fought the first open battle of the war and won it. At Badajoz,

Foreign Legionaries stare down the road to Madrid.

a mountain town defended by trade unionists, he met far stiffer opposition. On the afternoon of 14 August the legionaries attacked singing their regimental song. Losses were heavy from enemy machine-gun fire. At one gate only sixteen men, with drawn knives, held the entrance when the struggle finished. Yet another gate had to be captured before Yagüe's men were able to enter the town. In the open square before the cathedral, a terrible hand-to-hand fight ended with victory for the legionaries. An even worse massacre than usual followed. Many prisoners were taken to the bullring and shot; others were killed by the cathedral walls. Some were executed inside facing the high altar. A few days afterwards a visitor wrote, 'Blood had poured in streams from the pavement. Everywhere you find clotted pools.' Three weeks later Yagüe took Talavera, the last important town before Madrid. The Republic seemed to be crumbling before the Nationalist onslaught.

Mola could not move with quite the same speed. Many of his troops were fanatical Carlist *requetés*, very brave but not as well trained as the legionaries. His opponents, too, were in good defensive positions in the Guadarrama mountains whilst his flanks were menaced by Basques and Asturians. Before turning south at all he had to capture San Sebastian and Irun in order to cut the Basque communications with France. After ferocious fighting, watched by crowds of French men and women from their side of the frontier, Mola managed to take the town on 4 September. San Sebastian fell more easily. It was given up rather than let its lovely avenues be destroyed. Some Anarchists who wished to defend it were killed by the militia. Mola then moved through Burgos and Salamanca on his march south, only to be stopped by lack of ammunition and the well-defended mountain ranges in front of him.

The militia

On the rebel side trained generals gave orders to experienced troops who obeyed instantly. Within the wavering borders of the Republic the disorder of peacetime increased. Separate regions and different unions fought their own war, sometimes with each other. Despite the obvious danger from the west, the Catalan Government sent 10,000 men to assault the island of Majorca. They were driven off and the island was later used by Italian bombers to raid Barcelona. Elsewhere success or failure seemed to take place almost by accident. Asturian miners, using their favourite weapon, dynamite, recaptured Gijón. Near Saragossa a column of Anarchists led by Durruti spent most of its time shooting people and burning churches.

Nowhere was there a Republican army commanded by a Republican general taking orders from a Republican State.

The front line, often mentioned, was actually difficult to find. Usually it consisted of a fortified post on a hill in front of a village where the troops were stationed. Very little contact existed between one hilltop and the next, especially if it was held by a different union. When the P.S.U.C. sent a lorry-load of captured material to Barcelona, P.O.U.M. guards shot the men in mistake for robbers! Borkenau visited the Aragón front near Huesca during August. He found militiamen firing their

'All the younger men seemed to be wearing militia uniform.'

guns in the wrong direction; a regular army officer told him that the only likely casualties would be sparrows! Disorderly crowds of men, debating whether to attack, did not bother to line up before their commander. Some of the troops had brought mattresses so that they could be comfortable in the trenches. One 'soldier' turned out to be a girl who did the men's darning in the evening! Everywhere the trade union militias looked upon military ways as unnecessary, or wrong. Twelve hours' training was often considered enough to make a soldier. Such queer views were particularly common amongst the Anarchists. In their columns no man felt compelled to do anything; there were no ranks and no saluting! Six or seven hours might be spent in deciding what to do, by which time it was generally too late. Durruti was intrigued when someone suggested behaving like a normal army. He regarded appoint-

Ready for action!

ing officers and obeying orders as 'interesting ideas' but difficult to introduce.

A regular army officer, travelling to the front at this time, met some militiamen going the other way. Here is his description of a conversation he had with them.

'Where are you going?' I asked them with surprise.

'To Barcelona to spend the Sunday there.'

'But aren't you supposed to be at the front?'

'Sure, but as there's nothing doing we're going to Barcelona.'

'Have you been given leave?'

'No. Can't you see we are militiamen?'[1]

Side by side with such indiscipline went ignorance of warfare. In street battles such men were often skilled and dangerous. In open fighting they stood little chance against trained soldiers. Frequently they were surrounded without realizing it, or were killed because they regarded digging trenches as cowardly. Surprise attacks were often ruined by loud shouting. Sentries sang at their posts, abused the enemy or opened fire without orders. Once a detachment holding a position went off to eat grapes. When they returned the enemy was in charge of their sandbags and machine-guns! Most disturbing was the men's dislike of the few army officers who had remained loyal to the Republic. These men were despised and ignored. Their sensible advice was rejected because they were members of an army which most trade unionists had been brought up to hate.

The Republican Government, led from September by Largo Caballero, realized that somehow an army had to be formed, an army capable of stopping the lorry-loads of legionaries speeding along the roads or the *requetés* fighting their way through the Guadarramas. It would not be an easy task.

The defence of the Alcázar

Just how difficult it was going to be was shown by a famous incident soon after the war began. On 20 July rebel troops led by Colonel Moscardó had been driven into the fortress palace

[1] Major Aberri, in Mexican magazine *Hoy*, quoted in Bolloten, *Grand Camouflage*, Hollis and Carter.

The Alcázar after the siege.

of the Alcázar at Toledo. In this massive building beside the river Tagus, they were besieged by militiamen who had entered the town in lorries and taxis. Moscardó's son, Luis, fell into their hands and three days after the siege began the Republican leader Cabello phoned the colonel. Their conversation is now carved in gold letters on the wall of the room where it occurred.

'You're wanted on the phone, sir. I think it's your son, Luis, sir,' said an officer.

Moscardó picked up the phone. He was told that his captured son would be shot unless the Alcázar surrendered. To prove this was not bluff Luis was made to speak.

'Well, what's the news, my boy?' asked his father.

'They've just told me that they'll shoot me if you don't surrender.'

'Then you can do nothing but commend your soul to God, cry "*Viva España!*" and die like a patriot, Luis.'

'That's quite simple, Dad. I'll pray and then die for Spain. I send you a big kiss, Dad.'

'A big kiss to you, my son.'

Then to Cabello Moscardó snarled, 'Save your breath. The Alcázar will never surrender.'

Luis was shot exactly a month later. By then these words had become a slogan for one side and a taunt for the other. Day after day, week after week, the fine shooting of the defenders drove back the hordes of militiamen who tried to break in. Artillery wrecked the building; petrol was sprayed on its walls in an attempt to burn it down. Hidden under piles of rubble, living on dead mules and saltpetre scraped from the walls, these few defenders were unaware that they had become famous throughout Spain and Europe. Their world was a dim, enclosed one, rocked every few minutes by explosions. Iron discipline was maintained at all times. Between attacks, they held regular parades, celebrated all religious festivals and kept their one thoroughbred racehorse in perfect condition. After six weeks an aeroplane dropped a message stating Mola and Franco were near, but nobody believed it. Indeed, a priest who was let in spent most of his time describing the glory that awaited them in the next world!

As autumn approached the men heard what they feared most. Muffled thuds indicated that miners were tunnelling under the Alcázar's two towers. On 18 September a tremendous explosion wrecked the south-east tower. Its collapse was the signal for a desperate assault. Militia with fixed bayonets rushed across the ruins, singing and laughing. Had they kept moving, they must have broken in, but instead they stopped

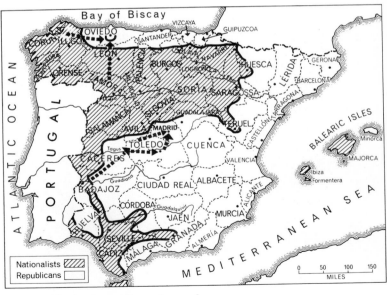

Division of Spain, August–September 1936.

every now and again to fire. Consequently they fell in hundreds. So did those who attacked from the south, although four tanks supported them. On the north-west side, where a tower stood undamaged because a landmine had failed to explode, seven Nationalists, throwing hand grenades, managed to halt the attack. As evening came the dead lay in mounds on the slopes of rock and wreckage but the red and yellow flag of the monarchy still flew. The Alcázar was as difficult to enter as ever.

By now it was a national matter. Caballero arrived personally to order his troops to take the Alcázar within twenty-four hours. Mining was restarted; the militia prepared to go forward again. On 25 September there was an ear-splitting roar as the north-east tower toppled into the Tagus. The starving defenders decided it was all over. They prepared to sell their lives dearly, little knowing that a few days previously Franco had turned away from Madrid to save them. From the military point of view this was unwise: every wasted day gave the capital more time to prepare. But his advisers pointed out that such a relief would have great propaganda value. In his practical way he remembered the arms factory at Toledo. Varela was sent towards the town. On the 26th all contact with Madrid was cut by his columns. Soon Moscardó's men saw friendly troops massing outside the town. As the militia's assaults had broken time and again, so now their spirit broke before the sight of the legionaries. Most of them fled in disorder towards Madrid. Those captured were mercilessly slaughtered. Next day Moscardó led his men into the daylight

Franco, Moscardó and Varela after the relief of the Alcázar.

after three months. Their eyes blinking, their faces thin with hunger, they paraded as if for a military tattoo. Their commander strode up to Varela, saluted and said '*Sin novedad.*'

The defence of the Alcázar was an inspiration to the Nationalist forces. In this happy moment, as cameras took historic photographs of Moscardó, Varela and Franco, they must have expected a swift victory. But what if the same spirit inspired the other side? What if thousands of men said, 'Madrid will never surrender'?

5   The Battle for Madrid

Foreign interference

How did the outside world react to these events? A peaceful
Europe would have tried to stop the fighting. Unfortunately
the Europe of that time was as divided and full of hate as Spain
itself. Germany and Italy were aggressive and warlike. Both
looked upon Radical-Socialist France and Communist Russia
as their enemies. To them the rebellious generals, with their
Falangist supporters, seemed the side to help. Republican
Spain was friendly with France. She showed no sign of sending
Hitler the iron he needed for his war effort. A Fascist Spain, on
the other hand, would probably be co-operative. The German
dictator announced, 'We must save Spain from Bolshevism',
and answered Franco's appeal for aid by sending Junkers
planes. Mussolini, the Italian dictator, had never been a
friend of the Spanish Republic. In 1934 he had secretly
promised support to the Spanish monarchist conspirators. Now
he announced, 'We must prevent Communism from establishing itself in the Mediterranean.' Soon Italian fighters were
protecting Franco's legionaries as they sailed across the Straits
of Gibraltar.

France favoured the Republic. She was ruled by a Popular
Front Government similar to that in Spain. Many of her
leaders were Socialists. With Germany and Italy unfriendly,
and with memories of what the invading German armies had
done to France twenty years before, the idea of a Fascist Spain
on her southern frontier horrified French politicians. She
answered the Republic's call for aid with weapons and aeroplanes when the civil war was only a few days old. Later, two
factors caused her to slow down such assistance. First, she was
frightened to become too deeply involved in Spain in case
Germany attacked her again. Second, she was restrained by
Britain.

Although her Conservative Government disliked Communists and Socialists, Britain's chief desire was to stop the Spanish

Mussolini, the Italian leader, desired great victories in Spain.

conflict widening into a world war. In August 1936 she suggested that no military help should be sent to either side. Such a 'policy of non-intervention', as it was called, astonished the Republic because it treated Franco as the equal of the lawful Government of Spain. Nevertheless, Britain kept to such a policy throughout the war. A Non-Intervention Committee first met in London in September. Germany, Italy, France and Russia all sent representatives. Since it was clear from the start that some countries were intervening, it spent most of the war restricting the amount of war materials reaching Spain, or the numbers of foreign soldiers taking part. Had it been successful non-intervention would have shortened the war considerably. Unfortunately Germany and Italy ignored most

67

of the decisions taken; in June 1937 they left the committee altogether. France continued to supply as much material to the Republic as she dared without offending Britain, whom she would need in any possible war with Germany. Russia, who left the committee as early as October 1936, helped the Republic also. Only Britain and the U.S.A. kept to non-interference, refusing the Republic help whilst Franco was able to win with weapons and men supplied by the two Fascist countries they were soon to be fighting in the Second World War. To a large extent, as the American Ambassador to Spain said, 'World War Two began in Spain in 1936.' Without realizing it, Britain and the U.S.A. allowed their future enemies to win round one.

Their attitude had another bad effect. Had they assisted the Spanish Republic its more moderate leaders, like Azaña, might have kept control. Spain might have remained a democracy. Because the only country prepared to help on a large scale was Russia, Azaña was ignored and Communists became more important. Before the war, in spite of what the generals said, Spain had been in no real danger of going Communist. In Primo de Rivera's time, for example, the Spanish Communist Party had been so small that he had not bothered to ban it. The 'Popular Front' Cortes of February 1936 contained only sixteen Communists out of a total of 470 members. The real revolutionaries in Spain were the Anarchists.

By October 1936 the situation was very different. Largo Caballero's Government was forced to send Spain's gold reserves, valued at £63,256,684, to Russia to pay for aid. Without the knowledge of some ministers, it was taken secretly to Cartagena, and shipped to Odessa. From that moment, as a Spanish historian has written, the Republic was attached to Russia by a 'chain of gold'.

The story of Russian interference in the Spanish war is a strange one. Stalin, the Communist dictator, knew Germany and Italy wanted to attack Russia. For this reason he had tried not to offend Britain, France and the U.S.A., hoping that they might help if this did happen. Communists all over Europe were told to pose as good democrats. Revolutionary talk was discouraged and 'Popular Front' alliances with

Stalin, the Russian leader, who told his men, 'Stay out of range of the artillery fire.'

Socialists and Liberals were encouraged. This policy met with a certain amount of success. By 1936 both France and Spain possessed 'Popular Front' Governments hostile to Fascism. In neither country was there an openly Communist Government likely to turn the western democracies against Russia. Communism was coming, under Stalin's scheme, but it was coming in by the back door!

When it became clear that Hitler and Mussolini were working to establish a Fascist Spain, Stalin adapted this peace-time policy to fit the Spanish War. If possible Franco must lose but Communism must not win either, because Stalin knew that Britain and the U.S.A. would never tolerate a Communist Spain. He also liked the idea of Germany and Italy being tied down in such a war. So began a coldblooded process of prolonging Spain's agony, of sending just enough aid to keep the Republic fighting.

To avoid frightening the British and Americans aid was sent as secretly as possible. Russian experts sent to Spain were told by Stalin, 'Stay out of range of the artillery fire.' No Russian troops ever fought in the war. Many Russians who did go as advisers and trainers were later shot by Stalin's orders, presumably because dead men tell no tales! Inside

69

Spain the Communist Party became far less revolutionary than the Anarchists or even the Socialists. Its numbers were often increased by shopkeepers and small landowners discontented because their property had been nationalized! The 'Red' Revolution feared by many would never happen if Stalin could help it.

Foreign Communists who came to fight Franco did not realize that the most powerful Communist dictator in the world wanted them to lose. Caballero suspected it and quarrelled with his Communist friends because they wanted the revolution slowed down. The Anarchists realized it when it was too late. It was a sad day for the Second Republic when the democracies decided on non-intervention. Forced into the arms of Russia, it spent its blood and money fighting the wrong battle.

International Brigades and the Fifth Regiment

As Franco and Mola's men advanced the Republicans issued appeals like this. 'Workers and anti-Fascists of all lands! We the workers of Spain are poor but we are pursuing a noble ideal. Our fight is your fight. Our victory is the victory of Liberty. We are the vanguard of the international proletariat in our fight against Fascism. Men and women of all lands! Come to our aid! Arms for Spain!' Here in a few sentences and slogans are expressed the feelings of most Socialists, Communists and even some Liberals when they heard the news from Spain. Tired of the bullying speeches of the Fascist dictators, appalled by the brutal invasion of Abyssinia by Italy the year before, these people saw in Franco's rebellion just another Fascist conspiracy breaking surface like an underground fire. In Germany and Italy few dared resist these dictators; here in Spain a democratically-led people was resisting. This is how foreigners, ignorant of Spanish history, saw the struggle, a struggle which seemed to offer a chance to 'do something' about Fascism.

During that hot summer as newspaper reports told the story of the rising at Melilla, of the massacres at Badajoz and elsewhere, a wave of indignation had spread across the world. In Britain a magazine conducted a poll and discovered that only five writers were for Franco whereas a hundred wanted the

Largo Caballero (third from left), Prime Minister of the Republic 1936–7, inspects his troops.

Republic to win. Poets, especially C. Day Lewis and Stephen Spender, wrote enthusiastically about the Republican cause. Spender announced that he would spy for the Republic. In a poem he declared that there was a bullet in Spain 'addressed' to him. Fortunately it never arrived! George Orwell the novelist left for Barcelona. Those who hated Fascism felt relief, like a boxer when the first blow is struck. Philip Toynbee, another writer, summed up the feelings of many when he wrote, 'the gloves were off in the struggle with Fascism'. To most, as one commentator has remarked, 'It seemed certain that in Spain Good and Evil were at last joined in combat.' Only a few thought the Nationalists were right. Like the generals, this minority feared that Communism would be established in Spain. Such a one was Peter Kemp, a Cambridge student, who went to fight with the *requetés*.

The driving force behind this help to the Republic was Communist. The first British volunteers to enter Spain were two young Communists, Nat Cohen and Sam Masters, who were on a cycling holiday in France when the rising began. The first Englishman to go to the front was a Communist student from Cambridge, John Cornford. The first English

71

person killed was a woman Communist, Felicia Brown, shot in Aragón on 25 August 1936. A British Medical Unit which went to Spain consisted entirely of Communists.

Such individual efforts were followed by more massive aid. Men and materials were soon being organized in a most efficient way. Inside Spain itself Republicans who were tired of the militia joined the Communist Fifth Regiment. Here was no undisciplined mob but an army as carefully trained as any *bandera* of the legion. Its leader, an Italian, taught his men to march in step by using the Madrid town band; its weapons and equipment were always the best Russia could supply. Each battalion was strengthened by a specially chosen 'Steel Company' who learned rules like 'Never leave a comrade, dead or wounded, in the hands of the enemy', and 'If my comrade advances or retreats without orders, I have the right to shoot him.' Nor were these orders ignored; of the first four hundred who went into battle only eighty seriously wounded men returned alive. Like the Russian Army, the Fifth Regiment possessed political commissars, as they were called, who taught the men the beliefs of Communism. This was necessary because most Republican Spaniards were not Communists. In battle it proved a fine fighting force and its units were later spread throughout the whole army to strengthen morale and discipline.

The most famous Communist organizations were the International Brigades. From a small office in Paris, Josip Broz, now Marshal Tito, the ruler of Yugoslavia, organized the 'secret railway', as it was called, which sent volunteers into Spain to form these units. The first five hundred left Paris on train 77, 'the train of volunteers', and arrived at Albacete, their training base, to find the floor of the Civil Guard barracks still stained with blood. Their commander at the base was André Marty; their first leader, Lazar Stern, who called himself 'Kléber' after a French Revolutionary general. By sea from Marseilles or by secret paths across the Pyrenees, these British, French, Italians, Germans, Poles, Russians and Americans passed into Spain via Barcelona and Alicante. Some came because they hated Fascism. Some came for adventure. All were determined to stop the Nationalists. Republican Spaniards gave them a tremendous welcome, offering wine and grapes, cheering, and singing the Communist anthem *International* or the Republican *Hymn to Riego*. It was like a new crusade, a call to arms. Another English poet, W. H. Auden, compared it to a migration of birds in a poem beginning,

> 'Many have heard it on remote peninsulas,
> On sleepy plains, in the aberrant fishermen's islands
> Or the corrupt heart of a city,
> Have heard and migrated like gulls or the seeds of a
>   flower'.[1]

The men behind the scheme, mostly old soldiers or tough Communists, did not see it so poetically. Like Franco himself, they realized that bravery and enthusiasm were not enough. During training Marty told his recruits why the Republicans had failed so far to stop the Nationalists. 'Why? Is it because they have lacked enthusiasm? A thousand times no. Is it because they have lacked courage? I say ten thousand times no. There are three things they have lacked, three things which we *must* have—political unity, military leaders and discipline.' Later he added: 'When the first International Brigade goes into action, they will be properly trained men with good rifles.'

On the morning of 8 November 1936 the XI International Brigade entered a Madrid already under attack from Franco's men. In corduroy uniforms and steel helmets they marched along the Gran Via, whilst behind them rode two squadrons of French cavalry. Excited Madrileños shouted 'Long live Russia!' to troops who were German, French and Poles! Perhaps the calmer ones saw in this sight more than just much-needed assistance. Perhaps they realized that the character of the war had been changed. Now it was no longer a Spanish quarrel, between Army and Separatists or the Church and the Anarchists. Now it was an international war, with foreigners continuing their own quarrels, on the soil of Spain.

' *They shall not pass* '

The Brigade moved into a serious situation. Following the relief of the Alcázar, the Nationalists led by Mola, Yagüe and

[1] W. H. Auden, *Selected Poems*, Faber, 1940.

Varela had continued their march on Madrid despite desperate resistance by the militia. With complete command of the air their Caproni bombers and Fiat fighters were able mercilessly to machine-gun the Republicans who foolishly kept to the main roads where they were an easy target. No amount of courage seemed able to stop the advance. On 17 October the town of Illescas, between Toledo and Madrid, was captured by Varela, who defiantly answered the telephone to the surprised Caballero. Four days later his troops took Navalcarnero. A counter-attack by Madrid militiamen, who arrived in double-decker buses, was repulsed at Chapineria

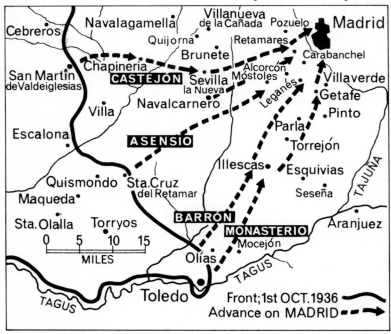

Final advance on Madrid.

and Illescas. Queipo de Llano, in nightly broadcasts from Seville, invited his friends to meet Mola and himself at the Café Molinero in Madrid. Franco felt equally confident, and began to make plans for ruling Spain after his victory. In a speech, he promised better conditions for workers and peasants although he pointed out that voting would have to cease; in other words, there would be no parliamentary democracy. He began to assemble lorry-loads of food for the hungry Madrileños.

This food was destined to rot in the snow and drizzle of that winter. Russian aid and the surge of feeling against him all over Europe were already beginning to turn the tide. Towards the end of October nine large merchant ships arrived from Russia carrying at least one hundred lorries, twenty-five tanks and 1,500 tons of ammunition. On 29 October these tanks went into action near Esquivias, smashing through Nationalist cavalry in a compact mass. For the first time Europeans saw the *blitzkreig* style of attack which became common in the Second World War. In this particular case, however, the Fifth Regiment infantry could not keep up. Left without support, the tanks fought an unusual battle with cavalry in the narrow streets of Esquivias. They were forced to retreat.

General Franco was worried by such Russian help. So was Hitler, who immediately sent the Condor Legion to Spain. Commanded by General von Sperrle, it consisted of forty-eight Junkers Ju 52 bombers, forty-eight Heinkel He 51 and Messerschmitt Me 109 fighters, some anti-aircraft and anti-tank guns, and thirty-two tanks. This strong force came as much for battle experience as to help Franco. Throughout the war German officers were to be found carefully noting the effect of this or that method of attack, this or that weapon. Air force pilots would disappear from Germany and return some months later very sunburnt from Spain; soldiers did the same. One man summed up the German attitude when he described the Spanish War as 'better than manœuvres'. Such help caused Nationalist confidence to return. Mola took personal command of the Madrid battle area, establishing his head-quarters at Ávila. On the same day as the Russian tank attack Madrid itself was bombed from the air. By 5 November Nationalist troops were in the suburbs of the capital and Getafe airport had been captured. Lisbon radio even announced that Franco had entered Madrid on a white horse.

Inside the city Madrileños had been preparing for a siege since August. A blackout, to prevent lights making an easy target for night bombers, had been hastily organized. Street lamps were painted blue with a mixture of water, aniline dye and plaster. Householders put blankets or thick curtains across their windows until the scorching heat of a Castilian summer made the rooms stifling. Then they left their lights off altogether and used candles. As the autumn nights grew longer Madrid became a frightening, ghostly city after dark. Windows were faint squares of yellowish light, often formed into criss-cross shadows by balcony railings. Lamps were faint blue patches which seemed to hang in the air. Few people went out at night. Traffic was reduced to militia lorries roaring madly down the centre of the road with blazing headlights. Occasionally machine-gun or rifle fire would shatter the silence as some nervous sentry opened fire at a shadow, or a suspected traitor was executed. When the bombers did arrive the tension grew worse. Shootings became more frequent, especially after Mola announced that besides the four columns of his army there was a 'fifth column' of his friends inside Madrid. All political prisoners were shot; when the governor of the Model prison tried to evacuate his to safety the guards suddenly massacred them. It became the custom to go and see bodies which were left at the place of execution. One eyewitness has described how 'the sightseers ambled from one to the other making humorous remarks'.

Besides such fear and horror there was great bravery. Although Azaña and the Government had fled leaving General Miaja in charge, the people were heartened by tales of help from abroad. The famous Communist member of the Cortes, Dolores Ibarruri, known better as *La Pasionaria* or 'passion-flower', made frequent speeches. Beating time to her words, this tall, well-built wife of an Asturian miner moved everyone by her deeply sincere Communist faith and indomitable courage. Throughout the war she was an inspiration to her side; the militia who died attacking the Alcázar had been part of a battalion named in her honour. Now her voice resounded through loudspeakers or on the radio, calling upon the women of Madrid to pour boiling oil on the enemy, calling on all workers to go to the trenches or demanding a fight to the end. To her delight, a regiment of women prepared to fight beside the men in the coming conflict. Monotonously the radio repeated the French motto at Verdun in 1916, 'They shall not pass.'

'Throughout the war she was an inspiration to her side.' La Pasionaria speaks.

On 7 November 1936 the attention of Spain and much of Europe was on Madrid. Elsewhere there was little fighting; in Catalonia troops played football. But on that day Mola, Varela and Yagüe attacked. They were already a little late for their meal at Molineros!

'Monotonously the radio repeated "They shall not pass."' Militiamen before Madrid, November 1936.

77

The attack on Madrid

As that November day dawned, legionaries in their green tunics, colourful Moroccan troops and khaki-clad Spanish soldiers moved carefully towards the river Manzanares. Above them, out of the morning mist, there rose the lines of Madrid's walls, defended by an armed population. So began a strange battle between a small well-trained army and the people of a great city.

The Nationalists approached mainly from the west through the Casa del Campo, a former royal park, although a diversionary attack was made on the suburb of Carabanchel. They

General Miaja, defender of Madrid.

had planned a three-pronged assault. Colonel Asensio's column was to capture the Model prison and the Don Juan barracks, Castejón was to take the students' quarters of the new University City and Serrano the Montana barracks. It was a roundabout route into the heart of the capital but from the military point of view probably the best. Unfortunately for Franco's men, most of this plan was known to the defenders because its details had been found in a captured tank.

Resistance on this first day was ferocious. Sheer numbers of militia overwhelmed the comparatively few Nationalists. Everywhere the attacks were halted. The following day units of the International Brigade arrived led by Kléber. They were spaced out on the basis of one Brigader to four militiamen. When the Nationalists switched direction and moved upon Carabanchel itself, their company commanders noticed the difference immediately. Instead of just wild, almost suicidal

Madrid under bombardment. November 1936.

bravery they were met by well-placed, steady machine-gun fire. The Poles, French, British and Germans were led in most cases by old soldiers from the First World War who knew their business.

At Carabanchel the only bridge had been destroyed. The

Manzanares itself was bounded by high walls which made it impossible for tanks or cavalry to cross. Moors waded through the water and started to climb the slopes towards the city. All day the battle raged in and out of this suburb. Skilled in street-fighting the militiamen found it easy to kill their African opponents. In the mist of that November evening Kléber assembled the entire International Brigade and with the cry 'For the Revolution and Liberty—Forward!' launched them in a fierce counter-attack. As the mist cleared, revealing a starry night, the awful battle continued in the parkland and amongst the gum trees. An army of shadows, illuminated occasionally in the fiery glow of an exploding grenade, grappled and screamed and died. Step by step the Moors and legionaries were driven back to the banks of the river. Only Mount Garabitas remained in Nationalist hands when dawn arrived to reveal the full extent of the losses. One-third of the Brigade had died. In Carabanchel itself fighting continued into the morning with hand-to-hand encounters in the Military Hospital. Otherwise the attacks had been stopped again.

With the battle swinging in the balance another Brigade, the XII, arrived on 12 November. So did an Anarchist column led by Durruti. Immediately he demanded that his men should hold a separate sector of the front. General Miaja agreed and gave them the Casa del Campo. Three days later these street-fighting experts were ordered to counter-attack. As they rose up from their trenches devastating Moorish machine-gun fire terrorized them. In one awful moment the folly of the Anarchist way of running an army was clearly seen. Untrained and badly disciplined they refused to move. At this crisis Varela sent Asensio's men into the fight once more. After three attempts they gained a foothold on the opposite side of the Manzanares. With the artillery pouring shells upon the Anarchists two Moroccan *tabors* and one *bandera* of the legion with fixed bayonets rushed forward. They had expected a fierce struggle. To their surprise they found that the Anarchists had fled. Within minutes they were up the hill and into the University City where they occupied two of the main buildings. The way to the heart of the city was open.

A divided city under fire

Madrid's University City had been planned by King Alfonso. It consisted of a dozen or more large buildings, lecture halls, hospitals and sleeping accommodation for students, each standing in its own grounds. At that time the whole area was unfinished because the Republican Government had concentrated upon building new schools. The great halls, some faced with white stone, some with red brick, stood derelict and almost unused. Builders' materials lay rotting in the sun; empty laboratories awaited their scientific equipment. And Alfonso's dream of restoring Spain's intellectual greatness with a fine new university was about to become a nightmare.

The entire area now became a battlefield. Each building was treated as a small fortress, to be attacked and defended, shattered by shellfire and bombed from the air, its walls splintered, its metal doors pitted with bullet marks. John Sommerfield, an Englishman who fought with the Brigade, described his first sight of such a strongpoint as follows:

'We saw the Philosophy building then, lit by reflected flames and moonlight. . . . The light shone through shell holes in the walls, from the windows the shattered sunblinds hung drunkenly awry, a wrecked car sprawled in the drive, and there were great holes in the ground full of water.'[1]

For ten days men fought from room to room and from floor to floor of these buildings, stabbing, shooting, shouting and running through the maze of corridors and halls. Mortars were fired down lift shafts, grenades were hurled up marble staircases or sent down in lifts to explode upon those below. Insults and curses in half a dozen languages sounded in the passageways, boots crunched on wreckage and broken glass, rifle fire boomed along the empty corridors, men used bookcases and laboratory benches as barricades. As gaping holes appeared in the outside walls, the November rain and mist seeped in so that the soldiers crept through a damp half-light. Every form of violent death occurred during those fearful days; some Moors even died from eating inoculated animals in the Clinical Hospital. By 23 November Franco knew that

[1] Quoted in *Civil War in Spain*, ed. R. Payne, Secker and Warburg

UNIVERSITY CITY
Ⓐ Science **Ⓑ** Philosophy
Ⓒ Palacete **Ⓓ** Architecture
Ⓔ Velasquez **Ⓕ** Agriculture
Ⓖ Medicine **Ⓗ** Sta Christina
Ⓘ Clinical Hosp. **Ⓚ** Del Amo

Puerta de Hierro
WALL
BRIDGE OF THE FRENCH
Mt. Garabitas
CASA DE CAMPO
WALL
Estremadura Road
West Park
Paseo de Rosales
Calle de la Princesa
Manzanares
MADRID

① Plaza de Moncloa
② Model Prison
③ Don Juan Barracks
④ Montaña "
⑤ Plaza de España
⑥ Royal Palace

TOLEDO BRIDGE

FRONT
Nov. 7, 1936
▲▲▲▲▲▲▲
Nov. 23, 1936
〰〰〰

Mile

Military Hospital
Lower Carabanchel
Usera Suburb
High Road
Andalusia
to Toledo ↓

Battle of Madrid, November 1936.

further attacks would lead to losses he could not afford. A whole army might be swallowed up fighting twice its number in such a maze of brickwork. Three-quarters of the University City, as far as the Clinical and Santa Cristina Hospitals and the Institutes of Hygiene and Cancer, were in Nationalist hands. So were most of the outer suburbs of Madrid. The rest was held by the Republicans. From then until the end of the war a divided country had a divided capital city.

Peter Kemp, who arrived at about this time, has described life in these suburbs. Different houses in the same street were sometimes held by opposite sides. His men, for instance, occupied houses facing each other across a road swept by enemy machine-gun fire. To keep in contact they built a 'tunnel' on the surface, made of sandbags roofed with planks, along which a man could crawl in safety. Here, amongst the pathetic remains of someone's home, furniture, utensils, an old violin, the troops played a dangerous game with sudden death. A sniper at a window might be bayoneted from behind, a unit blown up by a dynamite charge, or burned to death by flame-throwers which could reduce a barricade to charred ruins in a few moments. The sharp crack of a rifle, the evil chatter of a machine-gun, the tapping of a pickaxe below—all could mean death. A glorious assault had ended in a miserable game of hide and seek played by frightened men.

Although he did not cut off Madrid's water supply, Franco said that he would rather destroy the city than leave it to the Communists. Bombing attacks grew more frequent. The capital was no longer a city of shadows and dim lights. Now bomb explosions lit up the streets with blinding flashes. Red, green and blue flames made shadows writhe madly across crumbling buildings. On 19 November, when a thousand people were killed, the whole city seemed to be on fire. The hiss and crash of explosions, the cries for help or of pain, the clang of firebells and the shrill blast of whistles, mingled with the roar of falling stones and glass and the drone of low-flying bombers, made a deafening noise. Firemen trying to prevent fire from reaching petrol dumps and gas mains clung to ladders which stretched into the very heart of the blaze. Now and again one was hurled from his perch by blast. Ambulances screeched through the streets loaded with wounded. In the Plaza Carmen, a market-place, thick smoke and the smell of olive oil and burning fish made breathing difficult. At the San Carlos Hospital invalids crawled or fell from their beds to lie trembling underneath. The Duke of Alba's palace, full of priceless treasures, armour, books, paintings, was burned although militiamen saved what they could. In the dark,

83

'People prayed for rain and bad weather to keep the bombers grounded.' A fine day in Madrid.

foggy dawn people looked for their loved ones in the rubble. Sometimes they were alive; sometimes they lay dead under the soft carpet of soot left by the fires.

Madrid was the first European capital to be attacked in this way. Later, during the Second World War, most city authorities dug deep shelters. Being first, the Madrileños were not so lucky. Thousands slept on the pavements rather than risk being buried alive. Nobody really knew what to do. When a raid began they ran wildly in all directions. One old man told a journalist that when the sirens sounded he tossed a coin. If it came down heads he went to the right; if tails, to the left. A few days afterwards the journalist saw his dead body on the pavement. He had been killed running to the left and the coin which fell from his hand came down heads! People prayed for rain and bad weather to keep the bombers grounded at their bases. On clear nights, when the black stone city was flooded by moonlight, they knew it would all start again.

Yet the divided and ruined city was undefeated. At Café Molinero a table was marked 'Reserved for Mola and Queipo de Llano'. Its empty chairs indicated that the gamble of 18 July had failed. A long war awaited the generals.

6 The International War

'Spain one great and free'

There were now two Spains, Republican Spain, fighting for its existence against Germans, Italians and Spaniards, and Nationalist Spain, ruled as a dictatorship by Franco and his generals.

Franco was no longer the 'slender youth of delicate features and large shining eyes' who had gone to Toledo as a cadet. The man whose picture appeared on thousands of placards was described by a journalist as 'of medium height, handsome, dark-eyed and haired, with a small military moustache, and somewhat bald on the forehead'. From the Bishop's palace at Salamanca and later from a private house in Burgos, he worked a sixteen-hour day, trying to run a country and fight a war at the same time. The different desires of his followers, Falangist and Carlist, caused him nearly as many worries as the Anarchists and Communists caused the Republic. In the end he forcibly united them under his own leadership and imprisoned or exiled their leaders. His allies were not always co-operative either. The Germans thought his battle plans too old-fashioned and cautious, too influenced by examples from the First World War. Mussolini, thirsting for glory, demanded a greater share of fighting for his troops. Franco had to deal with them all, hoping that the money he had borrowed from millionaires like Juán March could be repaid, hoping that the Texas oil would continue to flow into Spain on credit terms. But though he might have to alter his plans to please his backers his ruthless will to win never altered. He was as determined to destroy his enemies as they were to destroy him.

Spain had changed a great deal since he had been a cadet; the very military academy where he had studied was a ruin. Franco's outlook had not changed. The stern attitude he had tried to impress upon his Saragossa cadets was now applied to

Franco and Mola meet at Burgos, 1936.

half his people. School children were taught that life was sacrifice, struggle and discipline. Adults, forbidden to talk politics in cafés, were told by him on one occasion, 'The old life, frivolous, comfortable, empty, must go. The *tertilia*, the coffeehouse table around which Spaniards have discussed their problems eternally instead of grappling with them, must go too. Such habits have been the cause of Spain's decadence.' Above all, Franco wanted a united Spain. Separatism was considered wrong. Catalonia, according to Franco, was 'as much a part of Spain as Lancashire is of England'. He was determined she should lose the freedom granted by the Republic. The Basques were conquered. The Spanish language was encouraged. Numerous posters displayed the Falangist motto, 'Spain One Great and Free'.

The Church was given back the privileges and power it had lost under the Republic. From the start it unofficially supported the generals, except in the Basque provinces. On 10 July 1937 its leaders announced that the Nationalist cause was the right one. Priests began to ask the Virgin Mary to protect Franco's soldiers in battle. When the shooting was over in a captured town the first action was to reopen the churches and celebrate mass. In schools religious education was restarted. Statues of the Virgin and crucifixes were displayed in halls and classrooms. As of old children had to recite the *Ave Maria* when arriving and leaving. All divorces were forbidden. Those which had been allowed by the Republic were cancelled. The Church influenced life even in small ways; at San Sebastian a modest bathing costume had to be worn covering knees, neck and elbows.

Nationalist Spain had some of the better land and was therefore well-fed compared with Republican areas. In Andalusia, the boastful Queipo de Llano, during his regular broadcasts, often smacked his lips as he mentioned the delicious meal he had just eaten. Evidently the 'radio general', as he was soon nicknamed, was not impressed by Franco's call to sacrifice and suffering! Radio Salamanca frequently used the same form of propaganda. Madrileños, about to sit down to a meal of chick peas or rice, were told of a Nationalist hotel where soup, eggs, fish and veal were on the menu. This was the first war in which broadcasting played a part. We saw how it was used to help the defence of Madrid. The Nationalists also encouraged their people with wireless speeches and reports. Good news was repeated, manifestoes read out and stirring tunes like the Carlist song *Oriamendi*, the old Royal March and the Falangist hymn *Face to the Sun* played again and again. Strangely enough, an important announcement was introduced by the playing of *Who's Afraid of the Big Bad Wolf?*

In a poor country made poorer by war little was done to create the better conditions for which they were supposed to be fighting. Just as the Communists became more important because of Russian help, to the Republic, so the Falangists swelled to 1,000,000 members as German and Italian aid poured in. The blue shirts of its members, its yoke-and-arrows badges, were seen everywhere. Yet Franco himself was not fond of Falangist ideas. At first he refused to listen to German and Italian suggestions that he should grant basic rights to workers. Probably he was glad that José Antonio Primo de Rivera was dead. 'The Absent One', as he was referred to reverently by Falangists, might have proved a rival.

The only attempts to relieve suffering were made by individuals. In Andalusia Queipo de Llano supplied 9,000 farmers with wheat for the spring sowing in 1937. Later he started a loans system for them. The widow of the Fascist Onésimo Redondo founded an organization called 'Winter Help' at Valladolid to help homeless and orphaned children. This was later renamed 'Social Help'. Its branches spread quickly throughout Nationalist Spain. Unfortunately 600,000 men were in the armed forces and all women between seventeen and thirty-five years had to do war work. Even if the authorities had wished to carry out drastic reforms it would have been impossible.

Jarama and Guadalajara

Until Madrid was encircled there was no hope of starving the city into surrender. During Christmas 1936 and early 1937 the Nationalists struck first north, then south, to try to surround it. To the north their attempts to cut the Corunna road failed after ten days of fighting in which both sides suffered severely. Gone were the easy advances of the previous summer. Now every mile was bitterly contested; the Nationalists lost 15,000 men and gained only a few miles of territory in this battle. Only at Málaga, taken by Queipo de Llano's army and the Italians on 8 February 1937, was there an easy victory to celebrate. The Nationalists carried out possibly the worst massacre of the war in this Andalusian town. Afterwards Franco described it as 'senseless shooting'.

The sudden switch south to the Valencia road, which occurred the day before Málaga fell, caught the Republicans off balance. Two International Brigades and units of the Fifth Regiment, commanded by two Communists, Enrique Lister and El Campesino, hurried to stop the advance. These two men became legends during the war. Lister had taken part in the 1934 rising. Of the Nationalists he said later, 'I don't hate them any more—it is an emotion too deep for hate.' Valentin Gonzalez, called El Campesino, the peasant, was famous for his red beard and fierce courage. He claimed to have killed four Civil Guards when he was only sixteen and to have fought for both the Spanish and the Moors in Morocco! A born bandit, he left his beard in a house in Seville before fleeing after the war. The battle in which these men were to take part occurred in the valleys surrounding the river Jarama, a land of rough scrub and gentle slopes covered with blossoming olive trees.

At first the Nationalists drove all before them. Soon their advance guard reached the junction of the rivers Jarama and Manzanares. With their main defensive line threatened, the scattered Republicans were ordered to stop a crossing at all costs. But at dawn on 11 February Moors crept silently upon the sentries guarding a bridge and knifed them one by one. Moroccan cavalry, their grey cloaks flowing in the wind, galloped across. The Republicans detonated mines which had been laid under the bridge for just such an emergency. It rose a few feet into the air, only to flop back into place. The Moors continued to pour on to the unprepared Republican positions.

Division of Spain, March 1937.

A French unit of the International Brigade was wiped out. A British battalion led by Tom Wintringham held on to a hill for seven hours, repulsing the thousands of Moors who ran yelling through the orchards, firing their rifles from the hip. As darkness came the dusty ground was still untaken but Wintringham lay severely wounded and over half his men were dead. Next day a Republican counter-attack supported by aircraft forced

89

Varela's troops on to the defensive. Moors dug trenches on Pingarron Hill. Americans of the 'Abraham Lincoln' Battalion swarmed and stumbled up the slopes. They were easy targets for skilled machine-gunners; they, too, lost half their numbers. Both sides were now exhausted. The Nationalists withdrew, after suffering their first defeat in battle.

'For them there would be no old age.'

As the Republic rejoiced the weary survivors sat amongst splintered stumps which had been gay with blossom a week before. One man, an American, wrote new verses for a popular song called *Red River Valley*. One was:

> 'There's a valley in Spain called Jarama
> It's a place that we all know too well
> For 'tis there that we wasted our manhood
> And most of our old age as well.'[1]

Kemp, the Nationalist soldier, fought at the Jarama. Afterwards he walked among the dead. Some Frenchmen, whose outer clothing and boots had been stolen by the Moors, 'lay there in their underclothes in every attitude, grotesque and

[1] Quoted in E. Rolfe, *The Lincoln Battalion*, Macmillan, Toronto, 1939.

stinking, shrivelled by two days' hot sun'. For them there would be no old age.

A month later the Nationalists came back. This time they were assisted by Italian motorized troops, fresh from their easy success at Málaga, groups with names like Black Flames, Black Shirts, and Black Arrows. The hero of the Alcázar, Moscardó, commanded the legionaries. Their objective was Guadalajara, a town north-east of Madrid, perched on a gently sloping hill. At first all went well; the great victory which Mussolini desired seemed likely. Suddenly, the weather turned bad with snow, ice and fog. Tanks and armoured cars slid on icy roads, or sank in mud as the ice melted. Nationalist aircraft were grounded by the fog. The delay allowed some Republic reinforcements to arrive.

A determined attempt was made to persuade the Italians to stop fighting. Messages offering rewards to those who deserted were wrapped round bricks and thrown into their camp. Actors came from Madrid to make speeches. 'Brothers,' their voices boomed through megaphones, 'why have you come to a foreign land to murder workers?' In spite of all this the Flames and Arrows pushed on and captured Trijueque. At one point Italians of the International Brigade fought against them. Then, on 18 March, the Republicans counter-attacked, assisted by aircraft and heavy tanks. El Campesino's men re-took Trijueque with bayonets. Russian cannon-firing tanks smashed the lightly armoured Italian cars and lorries to bits. For two hours this unequal contest continued. Finally the Italians broke and fled, so fast that Spaniards have been laughing about it ever since. Left without support, Moscardó's men had to retire on Jadraque. Mussolini was furious when he heard the news. He blamed the Spaniards for this first-ever defeat of a Fascist army. Franco's men, on the other hand, were as delighted as the Republicans at such a beating for the boastful Italians! In Salamanca his officers held celebration parties! The Italian Ambassador to Nationalist Spain became so depressed that he had to be recalled.

The Anarchist rising in Barcelona

With Russian tanks being knocked out by German bombers and Italians fighting the International Brigades it was clear that Britain's idea of no foreign interference in this war was having little effect. Nevertheless, the Non-Intervention Committee continued to meet, attended by both Italian and German representatives. A suggestion that the Spanish coast should be patrolled to stop war supplies from reaching either side was accepted by the Committee on 8 March 1937. The work was divided between the fleets of Britain, France, Germany and Italy. In addition nearly six hundred observers were stationed in Spanish ports to examine cargoes which did dodge the blockade. The scheme was not a success. The Germans and Italians spent their time looking for Russian cargo ships and so Republican aircraft bombed them on several occasions. When the German battleship *Deutschland* was attacked Hitler ordered her to shell Almería. These, and other incidents, caused Italy and Germany to stop patrolling in June. Aid still arrived for both sides. The Condor legion gave as much help as possible to Franco. Mussolini continued to call his army in Spain 'volunteers'. His representative, Count Grandi, said he hoped Italians would not leave Spain until the war ended. Such dishonesty reduced non-intervention to a farce.

Meanwhile trouble broke out behind the Republican lines. In Barcelona the Catalans had little to distract them from quarrelling. No Moors or Legionaries drove into their suburbs; few guns fired along their front. The ill-feeling between the Anarchists and P.O.U.M. on one side, and the Communists and the P.S.U.C. on the other, was able to swell and fester dangerously. The Catalan government, or *Generalitat*, was quite helpless to heal the differences. In May a quarrel broke out about the C.N.T.'s control of the telephone exchange. According to the Communists, operators were listening to their calls. On 3 May a Communist representative visited the building. His questions led to a misunderstanding and fighting.

Within hours the Anarchists had risen in revolt throughout Barcelona. The city became a familiar sight to those who knew its history. Paving stones were pulled up to make barricades, black and red Anarchist flags fluttered in the empty streets, machine-guns were set up on high buildings. The Assault Guards opened the churches and used them as fortresses. George Orwell arrived on leave to find the Communists controlling Barcelona to the left of the Ramblas; the Anarchists to the right. Death and danger lurked in every street and square. Trade union groups crouched behind sandbags, watching their enemies silently; a solitary rifle shot might start a fusillade which killed dozens. Two men carrying bombs entered the Barcelona radio station. They asked the announcer, an Englishman, whose side he was on. He replied, 'Yours'! In one street two Anarchist cars were ambushed by U.G.T. machine-gunners. As the bullets whined downwards the men seemed to explode out of their vehicles and whirl through the air, writhing like dancers. Once on the ground their bodies were shot to ribbons. Afterwards, according to an eyewitness, 'A small rain fell, and slowly, from each body, a red stain began to trickle over the square. The red stains met and ran into one another and soon the entire square became a lake of blood. The funeral chant for these dead and crumpled Anarchists was provided by the wild blaring of the klaxons of the cars they had so swiftly abandoned.'[1] After days of this haphazard violence 4,000 Government Assault Guards arrived by sea from Valencia. The Anarchists gave in. Their casualties had been very heavy, with over a thousand killed. The new world was turning out to be a Communist, not an Anarchist one.

Pleased with this success, Communist leaders now demanded the destruction of the P.O.U.M., a group which they particularly hated because it would not take orders from Russia. They produced documents which showed that the P.O.U.M. was in touch with the Nationalists. Not surprisingly, these later turned out to be forgeries. Caballero himself hesitated. He detested the idea of worker fighting worker. When he disagreed with the Communists about where the next offensive should take place he was forced to resign. His successor, Juan Negrin, a professor of physiology at the Madrid medical school, led the Republic for the rest of the war. This clever man's enthusiasm and courage helped to inspire his people to the last. He believed passionately that personal freedom would end if Franco won. To him the general's creed of rigid discipline, no freedom and enforced unity was repulsive and wrong. The professor's enemies claimed that he was merely a servant of Russia. They called him a Communist. Actually he was

[1] From unpublished memoir of Jaume Miravitlles quoted in *Civil War in Spain*, ed. R. Payne, Secker and Warburg.

Juan Negrin, Prime Minister of the Republic, 1937–9. 'He believed . . . that personal freedom would end if Franco won.'

neither. He knew he must use the Communists to win the war, and he was arrogant enough to think he could outwit them afterwards. Unfortunately, he could not do without Russian aid. Too often the Communists had to be obeyed.

Such a situation occurred in June 1937. The P.O.U.M. was declared illegal. Its leader, Andres Nin, was captured and tortured to try to make him admit he was a traitor. He proved too tough for his jailors and so he was murdered. It was almost a year since the different trade unionists of Barcelona had mingled happily in the Ramblas, dreaming that they were all united in brotherly love. At the same time another dream, that of Basque independence, came to an end.

Defeat of the Basques

The outbreak of the rebellion left the three Basque provinces isolated from Republican Spain. A circle of Nationalist troops surrounded them menacingly. These included their traditional enemies, the Carlist highlanders of Navarre, whose ancestors had three times unsuccessfully besieged Bilbao, the Basque capital, in the nineteenth century. Because of these past successes the proudly independent Basques felt certain they could again defeat any invasion. On 1 October 1936 the Republican Government granted them a similar freedom to that enjoyed by Catalonia. Under the famous oak tree in the town of Guernica, where the Kings of Spain had sworn always to safeguard the Basques' liberty, a Government called *Euzkadi* was formed led by José Antonio Aguirre. The provinces were by then not only free. They were absolutely alone. Off their coasts rebel warships patrolled to stop their supplies. The frontier with France was held by Mola after he had captured San Sebastian and Irún. In the Republic itself few Socialists or Communists were interested in Basque desires. It was obvious that the war would be won or lost in the south. Even had they wished to help there was little they could do.

Nevertheless the Basques felt confident. They were not born soldiers like the Carlists. They lived by business and trade. Their army of 30,000 was, to quote one of its men, 'a strange army composed of students, mechanics and peasants, led by a handful of regular officers'. But their own courage, aided by the granite ridges, deep gorges and high mountains around their territory, made them sure they could hold out. Bilbao itself, the second largest seaport in Spain, stands in a deep river valley. At that time it was encircled by forty miles of concrete and metal defences called the 'ring of iron'. Above all, this 'most Christian people in Spain', as a Nationalist admitted, were comforted by their Church. Here alone some of the priests were Republicans; here alone they marched to the front with Republican soldiers. The hatred of the fierce Carlist priests on the other side can be imagined. Franco and Mola, too, were enraged by the Basques, whom they looked upon as traitors to the Catholic cause. When Mola opened his attack on 31 March 1937 he was starting another bitter Carlist war.

None of his commanders underestimated the difficulties. Before the iron foundries of Bilbao were captured a hard campaign would have to be fought to a finish. Cavalry, tanks and even artillery would not be much use in such rough country.

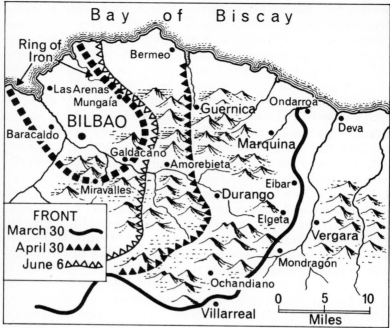

The conquest of the Basques.

The *requetés* themselves were also Basques who spoke the same language as the men they fought. Confusion in battle would therefore be worse than usual. To avoid it as far as possible, each Nationalist company carried a white flag; each man had white patches stitched to his jacket. Large arrow-shaped strips of calico were fixed to the ground to indicate the line of advance. At night flares and rockets were used for a similar purpose.

The battles which followed were fierce even for this war. Mola had announced grimly, 'I have decided to terminate rapidly the war in the north. If they do not surrender immediately I will raze all Vizcaya to the ground, beginning with the industries of war.' The Basques replied with a stubborn clever defence. They were short of weapons and ammunition, they had few guns and they were bombed ceaselessly from the air. Undismayed, they tied sticks of dynamite together and hurled them into the enemy trenches with a skill they had learnt playing pelota. They retook positions at night when there were no aeroplanes to stop them. They fought in the snow like white ghosts, ambushing the Moors and Italians easily in the wooded hillsides they knew so well. The *requetés* hated them and used dumdum bullets, which caused terrible wounds or else made little blue and red flames as they fell in the snow. Hardly any prisoners were taken. Even Basque stretcher bearers were killed with their wounded. Villages were captured, lost and recaptured many times. These 'unwarlike' people drove the Moorish legionaries back with bayonets, or grappled with them on the edges of high cliffs. Sergeant Yoldi, a Basque, wrote afterwards: 'We went on fighting because there was nothing else to do . . . we could not afford to retreat, because there was so little ground to retreat to.'

It was of no use. Superior force and better equipment caused them to be driven back. Courage was not enough against the resources of such an enemy. When the Basques won at Bermeo a Nationalist warship sailed up the coast and bombarded their position. Sergeant Yoldi wrote, 'For the first time I saw a whole mountain catch fire.' German airmen practised dropping masses of incendiary bombs on the pine forests, where they were hiding, or, as at Guernica on 26 April 1937, destroying a whole town so that it could not be defended. Probably no event of the war so horrified the outside world as this and it is the subject of a famous painting by Picasso. With large incendiary and high explosive bombs Junkers and Heinkel bombers flattened or burnt most of the town on market day. According to a

Picasso's vision of the destruction of Guernica.

97

Basque priest the sky was black with German aircraft which descended to six hundred feet. Farmers fled from their animals and lay in the gutters as machine-gun fire tore up woods and roads; burning buildings collapsed upon the crowds. When the raid finished 1,654 were found to be dead and 889 wounded. The centre of Guernica was a mass of flames. Franco still denies that this really happened. According to him 'Reds' set fire to the town before retreating. Hardly anyone believes this today especially as the Germans who flew the planes never made any secret of what they had done. A more sensible defence was that of Major Hugh Pollard who wrote to *The Times* to explain that Guernica possessed weapon factories which had to be destroyed.

Blockaded by sea, forced steadily back towards the coast, the Basques decided to evacuate their children to France, Russia and Britain. The Royal Navy had refused to let British merchant ships into Bilbao in case they were attacked by Nationalist warships. Only one, the *Seven Seas Spray*, disobeyed them and got through. Now, however, the British and French fleets offered to protect any ships with children on board. Basque children, unaware of the seriousness of the situation, were excited at the thought of going abroad. 'Can we have white bread and will there be butter and caramels?' some asked. Little did they know that in most cases they would not see their fathers again. A militiaman said to a British officer, 'Thank you for taking my children. We fight for the liberty of all, Basque and English alike.' Then he returned sadly to the crumbling front line in the hills.

The new offensive planned for 1 May was delayed by bad weather. On 3 June Mola took off to fly from Pamplona to Burgos. On that misty morning his plane crashed into a hillside and he died in the same way as Sanjurjo. Whether it was an accident or whether there was a bomb on the aircraft will never be known. Certainly his death was a relief to Franco who had found him, as he said, 'a stubborn fellow'. With his death the Monarchists and Carlists lost a good friend. Their influence was never the same again.

General Davila, Mola's successor, now led the attack. On 11 June his troops forced the Basques back to the 'ring of iron'. This defensive system turned out to be less effective than had

Part of Bilbao's 'Ring of Iron'.

been thought. One part was hardly finished. It was overrun by Colonel Sanchez's men and the way to Bilbao itself was open. Had the city been full of people a Madrid-like defence might have been possible. As it was the Government and the militia fled, after the Nationalists had fired 20,000 shells into it. On 19 June the last defenders retreated from its empty streets. After three unsuccessful attempts the Carlists had at last taken the city.

Basque dreams of freedom were over. Nearly three hundred of their priests were sacked. Some were shot. Schoolmasters who believed in Basque independence were dismissed. Nobody was allowed to speak the Basque language. Bilbao's iron foundries and rolling mills were taken over to feed Franco's war effort. In peaceful England, at Stonham in Lincolnshire, Basque children stoned the man who brought the news that their beloved capital had fallen. Some broke out of the camp and ran wildly about the countryside. In Bilbao itself a wounded Carlist priest, arm in sling, told his men: 'It is impossible to fight against God.' Abroad many could not believe that the Basques, of all people, had been fighting against God.

The Republicans hardly noticed all this. At Brunete, west of Madrid, and Belchite in Aragón they were busy launching full-scale offensives. Large armies became locked in combat under a blazing sun. Neither battle led to any important result. Both ground to a halt through the sheer exhaustion of those taking part; at Brunete 35,000 men died without gaining more than a mile or two of ground. Only the northern campaigns could give Franco any satisfaction. In August, the last important northern town, Santander, fell to his Italian allies. By 21 October, when Gijón in Asturias was captured, there was no longer a 'pocket' of Republican territory in the north. The Nationalists had the Asturian coalfields as well as the Basque ironworks. Their armies could concentrate on the one front line. Their navy was able to mass in the Mediterranean. The scene was set for the second year of war.

Communists take over

Inside the Republic life was hard and miserable. The destruction of the P.O.U.M., the tales of murder and shooting which were spread outside Spain by International Brigade survivors, the offensive which led to no victory, caused much of the early enthusiasm to die away. The flow of volunteers began to slow down. When men were shot or imprisoned by their own side, when an idealist like George Orwell narrowly escaped death because he had joined a P.O.U.M. column, there was obviously something wrong with this battle between good and evil! Gradually the International Brigades were filled with Spanish Communists, often ex-Fifth Regiment men. The days when men had 'migrated like gulls or the seeds of a flower' were over.

Supplies of war materials were slowing down also. In August 1937 Franco had become alarmed by rumours of extra Russian aid. He asked Mussolini to help. Soon Italian submarines were sinking supply ships bound for the Republic. Some of these were British and French and so Britain called the Nyon Conference. The Italians refused to attend and when Mussolini denied that his ships were involved someone suggested he should erect a monument to 'the unknown submarine'. The British and French decided to patrol the Mediterranean and destroy such mystery ships. In fact the aid from Russia was not really as much as Franco feared. Stalin remained cautious. Weapons still had to be smuggled in from any country willing to supply them. This led to many types of weapon and ammunition being used by the Republican armies and consequently to confusion in battle. An army equipped with six calibres of rifle, five of machine-guns, six of mortars and twenty-eight separate types of field-gun could hardly expect to be as efficient as one armed with standard weapons! Such handicaps offset the Republicans' advantage in numbers.

Behind the lines Communist influence grew steadily. Fifth Regiment units had been distributed throughout the new People's Army. Although this increased the discipline and fighting spirit of the Republican forces it gave the Communists almost complete control. Anti-Communist commanders found themselves dismissed; non-Communist units could not get essential supplies and offensives took place where the Communists wanted them. Caballero and Azaña were ignored and forgotten. The Cortes, which had moved to Barcelona with about two hundred of its original members, was ignored also. The Second Republic had ceased really to exist.

In Barcelona the Communists were in the position of an independent Government. Their secret police, the dreaded S.I.M., turned Montjuich prison into a chamber of horrors. Some cells were so small that a prisoner could not sit down; one had its bricks set on edge so that even to lean was painful. A black circular cell with a single light in the centre of the ceiling gave prisoners a horrible feeling of dizziness. Inside such places men were thrown into freezing-cold baths, or dazzled for hours with electric lights. Captain Lance, an Englishman, who helped people to escape from Madrid, was captured by the Communists and placed in a cell eight feet long and five feet wide. It was completely bare with white-washed walls, no light and a tiny window partially boarded up. Now and again he was taken from this semi-darkness and allowed a short exercise period. Since food consisted of rice or lentil soup and drink was warm water with condensed milk in it, the starving men often stole from the dustbins at this time. Every three days Lance was allowed to wash under a cold tap without soap or towel. He did so using his handkerchief. Each dawn a rattle of machine-gun fire indicated an execution.

Lance had tried to help Nationalist supporters escape. Communist authorities in Madrid spread a rumour that there was a tunnel which connected with the Nationalist lines.

Agents led people to it. As they entered they were shot. Sixty-seven bodies were found later in this 'Tunnel of Death'. No doubt fear was partly responsible for such brutality. Nevertheless, these deeds were a long way from the ideals of men like Azaña and the high hopes of 18 July 1936.

Battle of Teruel

Teruel is in Aragón, one hundred miles from the Mediterranean coast. When the war began it was captured by the Nationalists, who shot many of its inhabitants. From that time it formed a corner, or salient, in the front line. Here, where the frontier between the two Spains turned sharp north, Lieut.-Colonel Rey d'Harcourt's 4,000 men were surrounded on three sides by Republicans who could shell their only supply road. The town itself stands on a hill. All around stretch bare, treeless valleys. To the west a tooth-shaped hill called La Muela forms a strange landmark. In winter it is a bare, cold, miserable place. A grimmer spot for a battle could hardly have been found in Spain.

The Republicans decided to capture Teruel and so shorten their communications between New Castile and Aragón. They kept their plans very secret. Under the guidance of General Rojo, nearly 100,000 men were brought to the front line near Puerto de Escandin without the Nationalists knowing. They moved through the deep snow of early December in white clothes. Even their rifles and machine-guns were painted white. The Nationalists in Teruel were thinking about enjoying Christmas when this huge force fell upon them.

On 15 December 1937 Lister's division opened the attack. Within hours he had neatly isolated Teruel from the rest of Nationalist Spain. Then his artillery pounded the little town whilst his infantry fought their way in. The fiercest fighting was around the Convent of Santa Clara, the Governor's Office and the Bank. Soon these buildings were piles of rubbish with the defenders buried underneath. Republicans hurled grenades down holes. Defiant rifle fire boomed back from men whose water supply had been cut off. Meanwhile, other Republicans slowly fought their way to the mist-shrouded top of La Muela. When Christmas came men of the triumphant

'A grimmer spot for a battle could hardly have been found. . . .' Teruel from the Nationalist lines.

People's Army danced to the strumming of guitars before blazing wood fires. Their enemies starved beneath them.

Franco was taken by surprise. So ignorant was he of such vast troop movements that he had been planning an offensive far away, possibly around Guadalajara. He wondered what to do. This freezing-cold mountain town meant very little to either side in itself. Yet the general could never afford to lose in case his financial backers grew disheartened and stopped payments. So orders went to Varela to come to the rescue. Up the road from Valencia the Nationalists massed their troops. Overhead Fiat fighters and Caproni and Junkers bombers droned almost ceaselessly. The Condor Legion, just settled near Madrid, came too, grumbling about a Spanish general who could not make up his mind where he wanted his offensive. On 8 January 1938 came the news that Rey d'Harcourt had surrendered. Franco became more determined than ever. Teruel had to be retaken at all costs.

Whilst Franco planned his counter-offensive the worst Spanish winter for twenty years set in. Men who had roasted at Brunete now huddled against rocks, wrapped in as many blankets as possible. A gale brought on a blizzard which piled deep drifts on the roads. With the temperature as low as 18 degrees below zero, six hundred Nationalist vehicles became white stationary shapes. Guns and rifles froze into uselessness. The troops suffered terribly from frostbite. Toes and feet had to be amputated; a Nationalist general reported 3,500 cases in one division. Dead mules littered the roads. Men fell screaming to their deaths over icy, unguarded edges.

Somehow, in these frightful conditions, the Nationalists

counter-attacked in two places, at Teruel itself and a few miles north at Alfambra. Here their cavalry won a quick success, tearing across open country and taking 7,000 prisoners. In Teruel the Republicans were themselves besieged. El Campo-sino's troops fought on through day after day of freezing cold. Men clawed at each other in hand-to-hand fighting. Shells and bombs rained down until the white countryside seemed to be boiling under the bombardment. At night the red glare from Teruel's burning ruins lit up the sharp outlines of the hills. Slowly, step by step, Franco's men pushed the Republicans back until on 22 February 1938 they recaptured the town. El Campesino's division was the last to leave. The bearded warrior led out only eighty-two of his original 900 men. The victorious Nationalists found the bodies of 10,000 Republicans under the muck and rubble that had once been Teruel. Another 14,500 were taken prisoner.

So ended possibly the worst battle of the war. A clever attack by the Republic had been turned into a fearful defeat. Very few of the men who danced or listened to the guitar that Christmas survived. The ruin was complete. Peter Kemp saw Republican trenches completely filled with rubble after a bombardment, parapets that had caved in, pill-boxes in ruins. He saw 'nerve-shattered and tearful prisoners' being given cigarettes by his men. By contrast, he saw International Brigade men being shot by tank crews. Strangely enough, away from the battle area both sides rejoiced, the Nationalists because of their final victory, the Republicans because of their early success.

The war in Catalonia

The Nationalists, unlike the Republicans, were not temporarily exhausted by Teruel. Thanks to German and Italian aid Franco was able to launch a new attack on 9 March. Along one hundred and fifty miles of front line, stretching from near the Pyrenees to Teruel itself, his bombers and guns smashed Republican trenches, his troops moved forward. The result was a sensational breakthrough. Across the barren country-side of Aragón the Nationalist advance quickly became a victory march. By 3 April an important town, Lérida, had fallen despite a heroic defence by El Campesino. Its capture opened the gateway to Catalonia. To the horror of all Catalans, Nationalist columns began to wind through its fertile valleys. Two weeks after the capture of Lérida they reached the Mediterranean coast at Vinaroz. With cries of 'The sea! The sea!' dusty, battlestained men threw themselves into the rollers. They had good reason to rejoice for the Republic was cut in two. Catalonia was encircled, as the Basque provinces had been a year before. Now there was no longer a land connection between Madrid and Barcelona. Republican politicians had to fly over enemy territory to meet. Mail had to be brought by submarine. To Franco's men it seemed that the war was nearly over. Many started to plan for peace. The Falangists published their Labour Charter which promised the workers a minimum wage, social insurance and holidays with pay.

Barcelona was now attacked from the air as Madrid had been in November 1936. Savoia-Marchetti, Junkers and Heinkel bombers, operating from Majorca, arrived daily to devastate the city. They usually came in at high level with terrible results. On three nights in March forty-one tons of bombs were dropped and 900 people killed. Like Londoners a few years later, the Catalans crowded into the Underground for safety. On the platforms only narrow strips remained for passengers; all other areas were covered by people who sat or lay full length, eating, playing cards, knitting and sewing. In

'Catalans crowded into the underground for safety.'

the morning they wandered out, perhaps to search for bodies amongst the high piles of wreckage, perhaps to find their homes gone, or sliced in two so that their chairs and tables, their pictures and pots and pans, hung in mid-air for all to see.

The damaged city was no longer gripped by revolutionary excitement. Instead it had the dull, dirty, determined look of a city at war. Extracts from Negrin's speeches, painted on huge calico strips, were strung across streets from tree to tree, or from balconies. Walls and even pavements were plastered with patriotic posters. In the streets and open spaces young army recruits performed physical exercises or military drill. Speeches by La Pasionaria roared from loudspeakers as they had done during the first exciting days of the defence of Madrid. Always she was at hand to urge on the downhearted and encourage the brave. During a demonstration against a minister named Prieto who wished to start peace negotiations with Franco, her voice was loudest in denouncing him. Prieto, an old Socialist rival of Caballero, was forced to resign.

No one dared talk of defeat. Álvarez del Vayo, the Communist Foreign Minister, told visiting journalists, 'The Catalans would astonish the world, as was the case in Madrid.' He invited them to return in a month's time for another sherry! Negrin, scorning peace talk, summed up his war aims in fourteen points which he issued on 1 May 1938. Amongst other things he demanded complete Spanish freedom, the withdrawal of all foreign troops, separate liberties for the different regions of Spain and agricultural reform. More important perhaps than these words, he managed to persuade the French to reopen their frontier for a short time. Such determination and such a diplomatic success encouraged the Catalans. As far as possible they tried to live normal lives. Operas were still performed regularly; in all, fifty-one cinemas and nine theatres were open. Restaurant customers knocked off their chairs by bomb blast on one occasion were helped to their feet by the waiter and invited to continue their meal. This seemed to symbolize the spirit of Negrin and the Republic. They had been knocked down but not out.

Together with other supplies, the French allowed three hundred Russian aircraft to be sent to Republican Spain by

Division of Spain, July 1938.

lorry. Miles of trees near the frontier had to be cut down because of their wings. The Republican air force had always
relied upon foreign pilots and foreign planes. André Malraux,
now a famous French writer and politician, commanded the
International Brigade air squadrons which fought in many
battles. Typical terms for a pilot were £180 a month paid in
advance in his own country, £300 for each enemy plane destroyed, £2,000 for his relations if he was killed and £1,000 for
him if permanently injured. Such men lived a strange life.
They might be at a party or the opera one minute. An hour
later they might be diving low over a battlefield, machine-
gunning survivors, or spiralling to their death in a burning
plane. Civilian life was also a queer mixture of pleasure and
death, as the Second World War showed even more clearly.
Everyone was involved in a modern 'total' war.

Battle of the Ebro

To prove that all was not lost, Negrin's Government decided
to hit back. On the night of 24–25 July 1938 nearly 100,000

107

Republican soldiers, commanded by Modesto, an ex-carpenter, began to cross the river Ebro between Mequinenza and

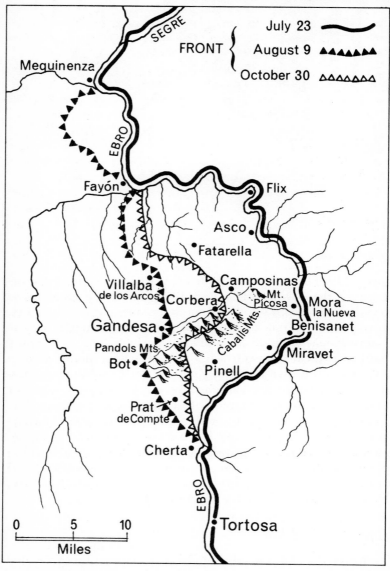

Battle of the Ebro, July–November 1938.

Tortosa, at a point where the river takes a north-east curve. Their first object was to sever Nationalist communications between the Levante and Catalonia. If this succeeded, they hoped to cut through the wedge of Nationalist territory which divided Republican Spain. It was an exciting, important moment in the war. With shouts of 'Forward, sons of Negrin!' thousands of soldiers swam the river or crossed in fishing boats. Five pontoon bridges were fixed in position to bring the heavy equipment over. By morning horrified Nationalists were being attacked by men armed with every possible weapon, including medieval spiked iron balls for use against horses. Taken by surprise, Yagüe's Army of Morocco fell back in confusion. In one day Lister's division advanced twenty-five miles. After six days the Republicans held two hundred and seventy miles of enemy territory. At Gandesa a fierce battle resulted in a Republican victory. On 1 August they took a Nationalist strongpoint, Hill 481, nicknamed 'The Pimple'. It was the first triumphant days of Teruel all over again.

This Communist-led army now decided to dig in and hold what it had gained. French engineers were employed to construct deep, well-hidden machine-gun posts. Two high ridges called the Pandols and Caballs were honeycombed with trenches. In the flies and heat of the third Spanish summer of the war the Republican army took up positions which could hardly be taken by normal methods. Behind the lines both Government and people were overjoyed, whilst gloom spread throughout Nationalist Spain. Would the Republic ever be beaten, men asked? Had the victorious march to the sea meant nothing? Yet as Franco prepared the inevitable counter-attack there were a few farsighted Republicans who realized that all was not as well as it looked. The Nationalist Army was still very strong and well equipped. The French frontier was closed once more; the Republican coast firmly blockaded by Nationalist warships. Supplies of essential weapons were really in too short supply for such a large scale offensive. Unless more could be found the Republic's only hope was to fight a defensive war, not launch expensive attacks.

The victorious Catalan soldiers knew little of this as they were urged on with monotonous cries of, 'Resist, resist, resist'. To them it seemed that they could hold indefinitely as Madrid had done. Franco himself realized that a frontal assault would cost too many lives. He decided on a technique made possible by his superior numbers of bombers and guns. A small area of the Republican defences would be systematically obliterated by a heavy bombardment. It was the 'big gun' methods of the First World War adapted for aerial warfare; in August ten thousand bombs a day were falling on the Republican trenches. The few Republican aircraft could make little impression on the massed squadrons which droned through a blazing hot sky. On the ground nothing could live in such an inferno of fire, explosions and flying shrapnel. Lister declared he would

Into battle.

shoot any officer who lost an inch of ground; there is reason to believe that on a few occasions this was done. But trenches of dead men were often all the advancing Nationalists found when they picked their way through the craters.

All through the autumn of 1938 this unequal battle of men against metal continued. A final tremendous push of the Nationalist armies on 31 October proved to be the last. The Caballs were captured in a night attack; the Pandolls by day. During early November shattered remnants of the Republican army began to filter back across the river they had swum in July. A campaign started in heat ended on 18 November as the first snow fell. The Republicans had suffered 70,000 casualties. Their last great effort had ended in failure.

Flight from Catalonia

As the Ebro battle raged important events occurred elsewhere. The Munich crisis of 1938 had ended with Hitler sending his troops into the parts of Czechoslovakia he had demanded. Stalin came to the conclusion that his hopes of friendship with France and Britain, the hopes which had caused him to encourage Popular Front Governments in Europe, would never be fulfilled. In any case, both Governments seemed unable or unwilling to stop Hitler. He decided if possible to sign a treaty with his most fearsome enemy, Nazi Germany. This astounding decision naturally affected affairs in Spain. Stalin could hardly continue to aid the Republic if his new 'friend' Hitler helped the Nationalists. From that moment Russian supplies, already reduced to a trickle by the blockade, dried up altogether.

For years the Republic's enemies had been demanding that the International Brigades should be withdrawn. Now Russia herself agreed! Negrin, for his part, did not protest. They had served their purpose in holding the Nationalists until a People's Army could be formed. Their discipline and training had been passed on through the Fifth Regiment to the whole armed services. There were few foreigners left in the Brigades anyway. Furthermore Negrin hoped that their departure would force Franco to send his own allies home. In fact 10,000 Italians were persuaded to leave by the Non-Intervention Committee.

So ended a stirring story which had begun at Madrid in November 1936. Almost exactly two years later a Farewell Parade took place in Barcelona. Silent crowds listened to La Pasionaria as she said, 'Today they are going away. Many of them, thousands of them, are staying here with the Spanish earth for their shroud, and all Spaniards remember them with the deepest feelings.' People wept at her words. Flowers fluttered down into the silent square. The last of the Brigades marched away. In London three hundred and five British members were given a great reception by wellwishers. Many must have remembered La Pasionaria's words and thought of the five hundred Britons who had died in Spain, fighting a battle which they believed to be their own.

As his foreign enemies departed Franco at last realized that he might never defeat his Spanish enemies without German

The conquest of Catalonia, 1939.

aid. Reluctantly he gave in to Hitler's demand for a 40 per cent share in the Spanish iron mines. In return Hitler started to send the necessary equipment. More money was borrowed, more oil flowed in and the Nationalist war machine began to move again. On 23 December 1938, 300,000 troops attacked all along the front. Here and there they were held back. Generally they were not. On the river Segre and in the foothills of the Pyrenees they poured through like an angry sea. Exhausted by the Ebro, short of vital equipment, the Republicans fought bravely but in vain. Lister held up the enemy for a fortnight until his army collapsed on 3 January 1939. Then speeding Italian columns carved their way through his re-treating, footsore Catalans. This time there were no Russian tanks to stage a counter-attack as at Guadalajara; no war-planes to batter the advancing enemy. On 4 January, when Borjas Blancas fell, only 37,000 rifles remained in Catalonia. A week later Yagüe took Tarragona on the Mediterranean coast.

In Barcelona there was panic. Years of propaganda stories had made people terrified of Franco and his men. About half a million began to trek to the French frontier. As they trudged along the bleak, high mountain roads, or choked the narrow streets of towns and villages, their numbers were swelled by those fleeing from the countryside. To the French officials it seemed that the whole Spanish nation was on the move. At first they allowed only civilians across the border. Later they said soldiers could come as well. In five days 250,000 Repub-lican troops left their country for ever, column after column of ragged men, still proudly defiant although unarmed and de-feated. Modesto himself led the Army of the Ebro into exile. The French were overwhelmed by such numbers. They set up camps but were unable to supply food, buildings or shelter. Men dug holes and slept in them. Less scrupulous ones ran-sacked French farms or cut down olive trees for firewood. Friends and enemies mingled in the confusion and at least one member of the S.I.M. was buried alive by his ex-victims.

With the victorious Nationalists approaching and no army to defend it, Barcelona became a dead city. Tramcars without drivers stood motionless in unswept streets. Starving mobs raided shops and air-raid sirens sounded repeatedly. One day a Nationalist warship sailed in and bombarded Montjuich

The end of the Republic. Refugees stream across the French border.

castle. Behind many shutters those men who hated the Republic counted the hours until Franco's men arrived. On 25 January 1939 Barcelona's long agony ended as German tanks rolled into the suburbs. This time there was no heroic call to arms as at Madrid. The long feuds and battles had broken the power of the Anarchists. Many Communists had died under a hail of bombs on the Ebro, or fled to France. Only traitors and the weak remained to welcome the first tank, on top of which sat a laughing German woman giving the Fascist salute. Shutters on balconies flew open as it roared past. Red and gold monarchist flags were taken from their hiding-places and waved. Below the *requetés*, a seemingly endless line of dusty troops in red berets, wound through the damaged streets. Here and there a band struck up a Nationalist tune. It was nearly two-and-a-half years since armed workers had taken control, determined to create a new world. Now the revolution was over and the new world was Franco's.

The fall of Madrid

On 1 February 1939 the Republican Cortes, first elected exactly three years before, held its last meeting. Driven from Barcelona, it had arrived at Figueras castle near the French frontier. Into this large, old building, with its moat and deep cellars, crowded the remains of what had once been the Government of Spain. Pieces of paper stuck on doors told visitors that this room housed the Ministry of Defence, or that room the Foreign Office. Outside in the cold streets the few people such departments still governed, mostly refugees, slept on the pavements.

In the castle vaults Barrio, the Chairman, banged his gavel for silence. So tired he could hardly stand, Juan Negrin rose to make his last speech to the Cortes as Prime Minister. His voice quavered with emotion as he told the members what they knew only too well. He described the course of the war; he explained how serious the situation was now that Catalonia was overrun. Bitterly he remarked, 'Our terrible and tremendous problem has always been lack of arms. We, a legitimate Government, had to buy arms clandestinely, as contraband, even in Germany and Italy. We managed to make some and scrape along.' He finished, the meeting ended, and the Government of the Second Republic dispersed. A week later Carlist troops entered the town. Two weeks after that Britain recognized Franco, not Negrin, as ruler of Spain.

Madrid alone held out, a lonely Republican island in a Nationalist sea. Inside its rat-infested ruins the condition of the people was pitiful. With just over a month's food left, and a daily ration of three ounces of bread per person, disease and starvation were killing about three hundred inhabitants a day. As in Barcelona, the Fifth Column of secret friends of Franco, nearly 40,000 of them, waited to reveal themselves to the armies which had stood outside the city for nearly two years. The Communist-controlled defenders of the Republic still manned the trenches, university buildings and houses, but they had few guns and in some cases no shoes or overcoats. About forty aircraft were available to hold off an attack by thirty-two divisions and six hundred aircraft.

In this hopeless situation, some officers of the old Spanish army decided that Franco might give better terms to them than to the Communists. To such bitter enemies his conditions had always been total surrender. General Casado felt that he

Division of Spain after the conquest of Catalonia, February 1939.

would be more lenient if the Communist leaders were dismissed. 'Only we Generals can get Spain out of this war,' he said, 'I can get more out of Franco than Negrin's Government ever can.' Consequently the war ended as it had begun, with generals rebelling against their Government! Within days parts of Madrid were in the hands of non-Communists supporting Casado. Negrin phoned the capital when he heard the news.

'What is going on in Madrid, General?' he asked.

'What is going on is that I have rebelled,' snapped Casado.

'That you have rebelled! Against whom? Against me?'

'Yes, against you.'[1]

It was almost exactly two-and-a-half years since another Republican Prime Minister, Quiroga, had picked up the phone and heard rebellious officers shouting, '*Viva España!*'. Even as it died the Republic was plagued by disloyalty.

This rebellion ruined the Republican cause at once and probably ended the war sooner. Yet Casado gained nothing. Franco did not intend to change his mind now victory was certain; 'I am not a weathercock' he remarked, meaning he did not change his mind like a weathercock spinning in the wind. Only fierce fighting resulted from Casado's plot. Like Barcelona in May 1937, the centre of Madrid became a battleground. One Republican wrote sadly, 'The streets of Madrid, which no rebel had trod, ran with Republican blood. . . . It was a miserable close for a saga of national heroism.'

Outside the city this fresh rising, plus the news that Negrin and his Government had flown to France, destroyed the spirit of the large numbers of men still under arms. Leaderless and despairing, they left the trenches, and wandered back into the city for which they were no longer prepared to die. When Franco's final assault began on 26 March 1939 there was little fighting. For some days previously Madrid radio programmes had been interrupted by announcers reading lists of numbers. People were puzzled, not knowing they were listening to code messages arranging the final surrender. On 27 March Nationalist troops started to invest the city. Most marched in but some entered by Underground and were made to pay full fare! The official surrender actually took place in the ruined Clinical

[1] Quoted in Alvarez del Vayo, *Freedom's Battle*, Heinemann, 1940.

Hospital, where the Brigades had stopped Franco two-and-a-half years before.

Fifth columnists were overjoyed. They draped their windows and balconies with yellow, red and white cloth or made themselves blackshirt uniforms out of any black material they could find. In place of 'They shall not pass' they chanted 'They have passed.' Ordinary citizens, sick of the war, also had reason to rejoice. Accompanying the Nationalist columns were hundreds of food lorries; in one day 600,000 rations were distributed. Simultaneously another far stranger army, of cats, was let loose. These had been collected in order to deal with the rats. As they ran mewing through the streets, as hungry people ate a good meal at last, as Communists were rounded up for execution, General Franco was told that Madrid and Republican Spain had surrendered. Without looking up from the papers on his desk he remarked, 'Very good. Many thanks.' A journey which had started in Las Palmas on 17 July 1936 was over. He was ruler of all Spain.

Death in action.

7 Peace

Spain and a World War

Now that Spain was at peace it was possible to assess the full extent of the disaster. First, and most tragic of all, there was the death roll. At the time it was reckoned to amount to one million. It seems to have been 600,000, of whom just over half were killed in battle. The remainder were executed or died of disease. In few wars has there been so high a proportion of executions away from the battlefield. Neither did these stop when the war ended. Behind the glamour of imposing victory marches through Madrid there was a grim story of shootings; in July 1939 hundreds were dying each day before firing squads. Franco and his men showed no mercy. Between 1939 and 1942 about two million people were put in prison or forced to work in penal battalions clearing up the war debris. Some of these convicts were guilty of crimes for which they would have been punished in any land. Others had merely made the mistake of fighting for the losing side.

Materially a poor country had been devastated. Although most of the important factories and foundries in Barcelona and Bilbao were undamaged, the farming community lost one-third of its land, machinery and houses. Nearly two hundred towns were so badly damaged that Franco's Government had to pay for their reconstruction. At least a quarter of a million buildings were destroyed, including one hundred and fifty churches. About a third of all rolling stock and locomotives were wrecked. The merchant navy had practically ceased to exist. Two facts completed this terrible picture. First, the Spanish Government's gold, if it still existed, was locked up in Moscow. Second, within a few months a world war began. There was no hope of help from other countries. The foreigners had come to fight. They could not come to rebuild.

Franco was placed in a difficult position by the war. On the one hand he was in debt to the dictators, Hitler and Mussolini, whilst France and to a lesser extent Britain were hostile to him.

On the other, war with Britain was unthinkable because her naval blockade would complete the starvation of his people. It was obvious that he must stay out of war at all costs. This being so he proclaimed Spain's neutrality. On the surface he remained friendly with the dictators. Large autographed photographs of them stood on his desk. Occasionally he made speeches in their praise. Really, the cunning obstinate Galician prepared to play the waiting game of his life.

That it would not be easy became clear in June 1940 when France collapsed under attack from the Germans. Hitler's Panzer divisions now stood in terrifying numbers on the Spanish border. Franco sent a message of congratulations and moved his troops into British Tangier. In his heart, however, there is no doubt he would have preferred Hitler's men to have been much farther away! Obviously it would be difficult to refuse Hitler's request for help in the future. This expected demand was not long in coming. Late in 1940 the German dictator asked for a personal interview. For the first and last time the two allies of the Spanish Civil War met in Hitler's own railway car at Hendaye on the French frontier. From the start they did not get on well. Hitler was excitable and moody. Franco was silent and obstinate. The Germans wanted a free passage through Spain to attack Gibraltar. Like most Spaniards, Franco had always regarded this fortress as Spain's by

'We must save Spain from Bolshevism.' Hitler speaking.

right. However, he wanted neither foreign troops on Spanish soil, nor Germans in Gibraltar. Perhaps he remembered what the Spanish people had done when a previous dictator, Napoleon, had been allowed to pass his troops through Spain to attack Portugal! Perhaps he recalled that Britain had taken Gibraltar whilst officially the ally of Spain and then never given it back! He agreed to provide fuelling and submarine bases for Hitler's forces; radio stations to spy on British shipping. Further than that he would make no promises. For ten hours Franco argued with the man who seemed at that moment most likely to conquer the world and against whom his own army would have stood no chance at all. The cold, calm Galician drove the excitable Austrian nearly mad by his silences and delays. Frequently Hitler was kept waiting whilst he slept after dinner! When they parted the German leader remarked to his friends that he would prefer to have four teeth out rather than go through such an experience again! Franco himself returned to Spain very unimpressed by Hitler's manners and behaviour.

For the next year everything seemed to go in Hitler's favour. Repeated requests for free passage to Gibraltar became harder to refuse as the German conquests continued. By the summer of 1941 Franco agreed reluctantly to a German plan for its capture. Fortunately for Spain, this plan was replaced by a far bigger project. In June 1941 German armies invaded Russia. This pleased Franco. He called for volunteers to fight against his old enemy although he still did not declare war. A 'Blue' Division of Nationalist Spaniards went to avenge the activities of International Brigades in the Civil War. Until 1943 they co-operated with the Germans, suffering heavy losses in the snows around Leningrad. Franco was doing his best to please what seemed to be the winning side.

By 1943 the Spanish dictator was not so sure. German defeats at El Alamein and Stalingrad in the autumn of 1942, the entry of the United States into the war, and the obvious collapse of Italy were gradually changing the situation. As Franco saw Germany's war machine being slowly strangled by Britain's blockade and bombing, as he received reports of the tremendous production of weapons in America, he decided to change his tactics. From the start he had offered to safeguard

'Hitler was excitable and moody. Franco was silent and obstinate.' The meeting at Hendaye, 1940.

British interests in Tangier. Now he became more friendly. American bomber pilots who force-landed in Spain were sent home. Thousands of refugees from Hitler's Europe were allowed to escape through Spain to Portugal. The two autographed photographs disappeared from his desk, to be replaced by one of the Pope!

When Germany collapsed in 1945 the Republican exiles in France and Mexico wondered what the Allies would do about Franco. Everywhere democratic people were condemning him as little better than Hitler. Britain and France called for his resignation. The United Nations refused Spain's application for membership. She was isolated and despised as few countries have been in history. But not a soldier moved towards Spain, not a bomb or shell was used to try to get rid of Franco. Republican hopes faded. This obstinate, ruthless man seemed as difficult to defeat as during the Civil War. As the war receded into the past it became clear that Franco had won his most important victory. Had he joined Hitler and Mussolini he would have shared their fate. Power came to him because he won a war. He lived on to rule Spain because he stayed out of one!

Uncrowned King

The defeat and death of the Fascist dictators reduced the influence of the Falange. Officially it is the most important

121

party in the National movement. Certain of its ideas, such as a united Spain with no regional differences, no free elections, but insurance against old age and sickness, were adopted by Franco. Even before the Civil War ended, on 20 March 1939, he received thirty-eight married couples who together had 342 children and at a little ceremony gave them the first payments of a special bonus for parents of large families. Since then laws have been passed which give workers paid holidays, old age pensions, sick pay and marriage grants. Nevertheless, although some of the ideas of the 'Absent One' have been adopted, although many streets are named in his honour, the Falangist leaders themselves have no influence to compare with that of the Church or the army. The real quarrels in Spain were old ones between landowners and peasants, churchmen and Liberals, and so on. With Franco's victory the Church and army had much power and the people and Liberals little. In spite of all the blood shed for Fascism and Communism little remained of either doctrine in Spain after the war.

Neither did the Carlists at first gain the monarchy for which they fought so bravely. The Law of Succession of 1947 declared Spain to be a 'social and representative Catholic State, which in accordance with its tradition is a kingdom'. Actually it was a strange 'kingdom' for no monarch ruled Spain from 1937 until Franco's death in 1975. Soon after the Second World War Franco reached an agreement with the royal family whereby Don Juan Carlos, the rightful heir to the throne, was educated in Spain. In the years which followed, he appeared beside Franco at official parades. On the twenty-fifth anniversary of the end of the war Franco said that Spain needed a new kind of 'social, popular and representative monarchy'. In spite of such mysterious statements, the old General was determined to tolerate no King while he lived. At Church festivals which he attended a canopy was carried above him like a king. He chose the list of clergymen to be promoted and presented it to the Pope as the old Spanish Kings used to do. Pope Pius XII awarded him the Supreme Order of Christ, an honour reserved for people of royal birth. On five-peseta coins is the inscription, 'Francisco Franco, Caudillo of Spain, by the Grace of God'.

This stern man ran his country as he did his regiments. Like his legionaries, Spaniards were treated well provided they obeyed orders. The Cortes could have all its laws cancelled by Franco; he answered to no one on earth. In 1950 he said in a broadcast, 'every enterprise needs a captain, and, as such, I am thoroughly conversant with your needs'. One of his admirers has claimed that he made Spain safe, 'not, it is true, for democracy, but for ordinary living'. The first part of this statement is certainly true. A Falangist who wrote the words of *Face to the Sun* was imprisoned because he dared to criticize the Government. Only one party stands at election time, only official propaganda is allowed in newspapers. Franco's own writings appeared under the name 'Macaulay'. Many intelligent men and women, particularly university students, despised a Government which was frightened of opposite opinions from its own. Franco's Spain showed clearly that Negrin was right. Personal liberty was at stake in the Civil War. Franco won and it ceased.

Spain today

Nothing would depress the dead Liberals, Socialists and Anarchists more if they returned to modern Spain than to see the power of the Church. In 1953 Franco signed a Concordat, or agreement, with the Pope which gave it more power than ever before in Spanish history. All education was under its influence. All its lands and possessions were free of tax. It received a large subsidy annually from the Government. Only its newspaper *Ecclesia* was not censored. Its power reached down into every part of Spanish life. Even some clergymen thought that this process had gone too far. As they worked amongst the silent and unfriendly population, some realized that the Church would be loved more if it had less power. This was the terrible lesson of the Anarchist Church burnings and the massacres at the beginning of the Civil War which was ignored by Franco. Under the influence of his extremely religious wife, he probably felt, just as the old Catholic monarchs did, that the Church was the one uniting force in a divided land. The history of Spain since the sixteenth century does not show this to be completely true. A Church which is the friend of the poor, as in the Basque country, can be a uniting force. A Church which is the friend of the Government merely divides Spain still further. The Abbot of a Catalan monastery complained in 1964 that the Church had done nothing to heal the divisions amongst the Spanish people. Spain, he argued, remained split between winners and losers. 'We have not behind us twenty-five years of peace but twenty-five years of victory', he remarked as the Government prepared to celebrate the twenty-fifth anniversary of the end of the war.

Spain certainly possessed plenty of 'losers' in every sense of the word. The great estates of the *latifundia*, whose owners supported Franco, reduced millions to the state of beggars. Spain is the largest olive-growing country in the world and over half of her population still toil on the land. Yet all this work and all these peasants, partly because of the unfair distribution of land, partly because of the frosts and droughts which have plagued Spain since the war, produced only 38 per cent of the national income. In recent years there have been attempts to improve such people's lives but in 1956 only 100,000 people owned cars in a country of 30,000,000. Occasionally there is talk of agricultural reform on a large scale. Actually Spain's rulers are still trying aspirins to cure an appendicitis!

Industrial workers and miners are far better off, although they find that when the government decrees a rise in wages, prices in shops rise as well. The Franco system of organizing workers and managers into syndicates, or unions, which are directly controlled by the Government, was deeply resented. In March 1964 Madrid police had to disperse marching students who protested at being forced to join the state-controlled education syndicate. They demanded free unions. The same month saw disturbances at a national syndical congress attended by Franco himself. A Government official was forced to appeal for unity. He condemned the old type of unions, which, he claimed, caused the Civil War. The young men were not satisfied, especially as many would have known little about the old C.N.T. or U.G.T.

Undoubtedly Spain's living standards improved as her isolation from the outside world dwindled. From 1950 onwards she was admitted to most of the United Nations organizations. The turning-point came in 1953, after the dreadful years of suffering following the war. The Americans were allowed to build three bomber bases on Spanish soil for use against Russia if necessary, as well as a naval base and an early warning system on Majorca. In return American money began to arrive to relieve the starvation. Between that time and the renewal of the agreement in 1963 Spaniards received over £70,000,000 worth of aid. Franco, of course, acted in a proudly Spanish way over this. The Stars and Stripes do not fly over the bases, which are officially commanded by Spaniards. The hatred of foreign interference, dating back to the days of Napoleon, is as strong as ever. But whether they fly foreign flags or not, such bases mean that Spain is part of the western defence plan.

There are signs that this aid will help Spain's poverty to disappear. Since 1953 the country has been 'discovered' by tourists; over 10,000,000 spent holidays there in 1963. On the industrial side, the government attempted to modernise the country. Many houses were built, railways improved and a large hydro-electric plant completed. Entry into the Common Market would probably help, but Spain's application has been refused due to the influence of Socialists in Italy and Belgium. If the Government is really serious, if a genuine attempt is made to cure Spain's poverty and backwardness, the old revolutionary desires, so beaten and crushed in the Civil War, may die away altogether. Certainly the miners and workers of today usually strike for better conditions and not for the old dreams of anarchy. The madness of those earlier Spaniards may be a thing of the past. But separatists from the Basque region still kill policemen and try to blow up politicians. Forced underground, the opposition is becoming ever more violent.

The man who won

Franco lived in the sixteenth-century royal palace of El Pardo, fourteen miles from Madrid. This white granite building, decorated with pointed towers, stands amongst miles of lovely forest land, filled with wandering herds of deer. Fold after fold of land is covered with trees; they stretch to the first slopes of the Guadarrama mountains, hazy and blue in the distance. Here the man whose enemies once held these hills went shooting and fishing. In the grounds are tennis courts, a swimming pool and a little cottage where he enjoyed privacy.

Did he ever think of the past? Did he think of all the enemies he outlived? Azaña who died in France, Companys whom he had shot, the intellectual Negrin, or Caballero, whose spirit was broken by years in a German concentration camp? Did he think of the years of struggle and horror which led him to this quiet spot? Probably not. For life presented enough problems; it was not all pleasure and peace. Franco usually got up at nine o'clock and after a light breakfast worked until lunch-time, which in Spain is after 2 p.m. There followed the traditional Spanish rest in the afternoon and then work from five until ten at night. At midnight the man who fought a 'crusade' to rid Spain of the Church's enemies used to say his prayers with his wife before he went to bed.

Unlike Hitler or Mussolini, Franco had no desire to strut and boast in front of crowds. Very few biographies of him have been written. Even a book he wrote when a young officer in Morocco has been out of print for years. When he did appear in public he was well protected. Twenty or thirty soldiers, wearing red Carlist berets, guarded him with tommy-guns at the ready. His Rolls-Royce was bullet-proof. At parades his Moorish guards rode on horseback beside him. Plain-clothes detectives mingled with the spectators. Yet vast crowds gathered to mourn his death in November 1975.

Spanish feelings towards him were a strange mixture. Herbert Matthews, a reporter during the war, has written: 'Franco achieved the extraordinary position of being, on the whole, neither hated nor loved in Spain. To those who know the Spaniards, this is the highest form of condemnation.' At the end of the war he was regarded as a cautious, second-rate general who had needed foreign help to defeat his own people, as a ruthless friend of the rich and powerful. His achievements in keeping Spain out of the Second World War and gaining American aid without giving much away caused some people to respect him. Towards the end this excitable race usually looked upon their ice-cold leader as very dull, very old-fashioned. They amused themselves by making up jokes about him. To do so probably meant that they regarded him as a fixture, an institution. The little Galician cared little one way or the other. A man who grew up in the Moroccan war was hardly likely to worry about a few jokes!

Valley of the Fallen

Thirty-two miles from Madrid stands a stone cross five hundred feet high. It is hollow and inside lifts carry sightseers up as far as the two giant arms. At night it is floodlit and can be seen from the capital. It stands within sight of the Guadarrama mountains, near where Mola's columns were halted in what seemed an easy march and held for nearly three years. Here thousands of men gazed upon the earth for the last time.

Four large statues of the Apostles flank each foot of the cross. Underneath is a crypt seven hundred feet long. Within it is chill and gloomy because the walls are of grey granite. Three side-chapels, dedicated to each of the Nationalist armies, lead off from this chamber. Niches, like small rooms, line the walls but they house no bodies. Above, a domed roof of dazzling brightness compensates for the greyness below. In the centre a huge statue of Christ dominates smaller figures of the Spanish saints. This is the monument which Franco constructed in the Valley of the Fallen. At first only the body of

'To the Dead.' Franco's Tomb

José Antonio Primo de Rivera rested there. Outside the area became a cemetery for the casualties from both sides.

In 1975 Franco himself was buried beside the founder of the Falange. This monument means something different to those who experienced the war, to one a hated sign of defeat, to another a symbol of victory, to many a reminder of a loved one who marched away and never returned. Certainly it will stand lonely and silent when every heart which suffered pain and misery during the war is still, and a generation which never knew the madness of those July days in 1936 has learned to live together in peace and perhaps freedom.

Further Reading

FRANZ BORKENAU: *The Spanish Cockpit*. Faber, 1937.

GERALD BRENAN: *The Spanish Labyrinth*. Cambridge, 1943.

JAMES CLEUGH: *Spanish Fury*. Harrap, 1962.

S. F. A. COLES: *Franco of Spain*. Spearman, 1954.

ERNEST HEMINGWAY: *For Whom the Bell Tolls*. Scribner, 1940.

PETER KEMP. *Mine Were of Trouble*.

SALVADOR DE MADARIAGA: *Spain*. Benn, 1930; Cape, new edn., 1942.

PETER MERIN: *Spain Between Death and Birth*, trans. by C. Fullman, Lane, 1938.

MALCOLM MUGGERIDGE: *The Thirties*. Hamish Hamilton, 1940.

A. RAMOS OLIVEIRA: *Politics, Economics and Man of Modern Spain*. Gollancz, 1946.

GEORGE ORWELL: *Homage to Catalonia*. Secker & Warburg, 1938; Penguin, 1962.

E. ALISON PEERS: *The Spanish Tragedy, 1930–1936*. Methuen, 1936.

E. ROLFE: *The Lincoln Battalion*. Random House; Macmillan, Toronto, 1939.

STEPHEN SPENDER AND JOHN LEHMANN: *Poems for Spain*. Hogarth, 1939.

HUGH THOMAS: *The Spanish Civil War*. Eyre & Spottiswoode, 1961.

Who was Who

For the Republic

Spanish Communist Party.
C.N.T. Anarchist trade unions.
F.A.I. Anarchist Secret Society.
P.O.U.M. Communist group against Russia.
U.G.T. Socialist trade unions.
P.S.U.C. Socialist-Communist party of Catalonia.
Basque Nationalist party.
Assault Guards.
International Brigades.
The Fifth Regiment.

LEADERS AND SOLDIERS

Manuel Azaña. President of the Spanish Republic.
Largo Caballero. Prime Minister 1936–7.
Casares Quiroga. Republican Prime Minister before war.
Juan Negrin. Prime Minister 1937–9.
Luis Companys. President of Catalonia.
José Aguirre. President of the Basque Republic.
Alvarez del Vayo. Foreign Minister, Spanish Republic.
Bueneventura Durruti. Anarchist leader.
Indalecio Prieto. Socialist politician.
Martinez Barrio. Republican politician.
Enrique Lister. Republican general.
El Campesino. Republican General.
Vicente Rojo. Chief of Staff, Republican Army.
Guilloto Modesto. Republican general.
José Miaja. Republican General.
André Marty. Trainer of International Brigades.
Lazar Stern (General Kléber). International Brigade commander.
La Pasionaria (Dolores Ibarruri). Communist politician.

For the Nationalists

Spanish Church (except for Basque areas).
C.E.D.A. Catholic Political Party.
J.O.N.S. Spanish Fascist Party.
Falange Española. Falangist Party (later joined Fascist J.O.N.S.).
U.M.E. Army officers' group against Republic.
Requetés. Carlist armies.
Civil Guards.
Monarchists. (These were often Carlists.)

LEADERS AND SOLDIERS

Francisco Franco. Commander-in-Chief and Head of State.
Gil Robles. Leader of C.E.D.A.
Calvo Sotelo. Monarchist. Murdered before war.
Emilio Mola. Nationalist general.
Millán Astray. Nationalist general. Founder of Foreign Legion.
José Antonio Primo de Rivera. Founder of Falange.
José Varela. Nationalist general.
Juan Yagüe. Nationalist general.
Onésimo Redondo. Founder of J.O.N.S.
Fidel Davila. Nationalist general.
Moscardó Ituarte. Nationalist general. Defender of Alcázar.
Manuel Goded. Nationalist general.
José Sanjurjo. Nationalist general. Killed at outbreak of war.
Queipo de Llano. Nationalist general.
Asensio Cabanillas. Nationalist general. [General of same name fought for Republic.]
Castejon Espinosa. Nationalist general.
Joaquin Fanjul. Nationalist general.

Index